Furniture by Design

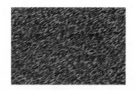

# Furniture by Design

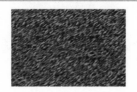

*Design, Construction, & Technique*

Written and Illustrated by
## Graham Blackburn

Lyons & Burford, Publishers

Copyright © 1997 by Graham Blackburn

ALL RIGHTS RESERVED. No part of this book may be reproduced in any manner without the express written consent of the publisher, except in the case of brief excerpts in critical reviews and articles. All inquiries should be addressed to: Lyons & Burford, Publishers, 31 West 21 Street, New York, NY 10010.

Design by Joel Friedlander Publishing Services

Printed in the United States of America

10 9 8 7 6 5 4 3 2 1

**Library of Congress Cataloging-in-Publication Data**
Blackburn, Graham, 1940–
        Furniture by design: design, construction & technique / Graham
Blackburn.
                p.  cm.
        Includes index.
        ISBN 1-55821-512-3
        1. Furniture making—Amateurs' manuals.  2. Furniture design—
Amateurs' manuals.  I. Title.
    TT195.B5797   1996
    684.1—dc21                                    96-48141
                                                  CIP

# Contents

# Acknowledgments

Grateful acknowledgment is made to the magazine *Woodwork,* in which articles substantially similar to chapters 1, 2, 3, 4, 6, 7, 9, 11, 12, and 13 first appeared; to the magazine *Popular Woodworking,* in which much of chapters 5 and 8 first appeared; and to the magazine *Fine Woodworking* for much of the material in chapter 10.

# Introduction

*Producing your own designs*

Woodworking as a hobby is admirably served by a wealth of books on tools, joints, joinery, construction, and published plans and projects. Insofar as many people are drawn to woodworking primarily by the desire to make some sawdust, use some tools, or simply enjoy the smell and feel of one of nature's most beautiful and versatile materials, this is fine. What is egregiously overlooked, however, is one aspect of the very reason for the craft in the first place: the designing of utilitarian objects with as much beauty as possible. Furniture does not exist to make woodworking possible; woodworking is the result of the need to make—and design—furniture. The design part is most often neglected and consequently remains a mystery to many woodworkers, who are then forced to rely on other people's designs if they wish to practice a craft at once venerable and completely contemporary.

If you want freedom from someone else's plans and the ability to produce furniture that has no exact counterpart in published projects and cutting lists, then you need to understand how designs are arrived at.

Design consists of arranging pleasing shapes and fulfilling specific needs. Furniture that is to be primarily utilitarian is largely designed according to the dictum "form follows function." If the bookcase must hold a hundred books, it needs to be a certain minimum size. If the table must seat sixteen, you cannot get by with something that measures only 4 feet by 4 feet. You start with these givens and try to produce something that works and looks good.

As a woodworker, there is another element to the design problem: You have to be able to figure out how to build the piece. This is not just a question of knowing how to operate whatever machinery you own or use whatever tools you have to construct the design, but also of how to apply this knowledge to the design in question.

How you make things will also affect the design. Although you should not fall into the trap of designing only things that you have the technical ability to produce—you will never learn anything more unless you challenge yourself occasionally—it is patently pointless to attempt a project that possesses problems for which there is no imaginable solution.

The French Art Nouveau designer Ruhlmann was famous for pieces that included elements no one had attempted before. He was fortunate in having his own master cabinetmaker to figure out how these designs might be realized. Together these two masters produced wonderful new designs. You must be both people. Consequently, each project must be considered in the light of three questions: What do I want the piece to do? How do I want it to look? How can it be made?

The projects that follow address these concerns, sometimes focusing on one element, sometimes on another, and sometimes examining how all three interact to produce the end result. The subtitles of each chapter indicate which aspects of design are exemplified by the subject piece. Cutting lists, where given, represent dimensions of the illustrated pieces and as such are intended primarily as a guide from which overall proportions can be ascertained. You should regard them only as a jumping-off point for similar pieces of different sizes that may suit your purposes better.

The sequence of the lessons that will be learned by attempting the projects—or your own adaptations of the projects—in this book proceeds from the general to the specific and, for the most part, from the simple to the complicated. Chapter 1 provides an introduction to the awareness required to design intelligently and illustrates the different needs that should be considered when trying to decide on stylistic concerns. Thereafter, each chapter may be read in whatever order your prefer. While there is a certain amount of referring to points made in previous chapters, each chapter nevertheless constitutes a stand-alone project elucidating one or more questions of design.

# Television cabinet

*The importance of design*

Nine times out of ten the first thing that strikes you when you look at a piece of furniture is the design. The shape, the proportions, and the color are what you notice first. As a woodworker, you then undoubtedly get closer to investigate how the piece was put together, usually with a critical eye to the exactness of the joinery and the niceness of the finish. For many people the technical considerations are everything; their assessment of a piece is based solely on the maker's technical skill. These are not necessarily bad reactions, but they ignore another extremely important element in a piece's overall success or failure: its design. The elements of joinery are there for all to see, while the elements of the design—all those small but important decisions that were made along the way—are lost in the effect of the finished whole. It is much harder to trace the importance of the exact width of a stile or a rail, in relation to overall length, than it is to see how closely two surfaces are joined. And even if attention is paid to issues of design, the logic behind their creation can be missed by the untrained eye.

It is a big step toward becoming a successful furniture maker when you start to ask questions about the internal proportions of a piece as well as its overall dimensions. But these answers are harder to find than are those to technical questions. They tend to be buried in generalizations found in books on design theory and art history. It is often difficult for a beginner to relate purely theoretical ideas to the piece at hand. This chapter explains the logic behind the design of a television cabinet; the process can be applied to numerous other projects as well.

You should always bear in mind the design of a piece and its constituent parts. Even if you are working from plans, no matter how detailed, there will always be decisions to be made that will affect whether the finished piece looks "right." This is meant in an aesthetic sense: Does the piece have soul, a sense of balance, a feeling of fitness or grace? Is it charming, assertive, or intrusive, or does it just sit there, nondescript, evoking no emotional response whatsoever?

Paying attention to grain direction is an obvious example of how small decisions can affect the finished piece. The joinery may be perfect and the plans may have been followed exactly, but if the grain of the various parts is not complementary, the piece will not be as successful as it might have been.

The ability to appreciate the differences such decisions can make is in almost everyone, even if the reasons are not clearly understood. If the piece has been built with aesthetic as well as technical care, people will be moved to talk about its "sublime beauty" for lack of the ability to recognize what constitutes the foundation of that beauty. Rarely is sublime beauty fortuitous; the bricks and mortar of all the small internal design considerations will have been laid with great care.

**Design versus givens**—There are usually certain "givens" with any project. These may appear complete as when, for example, you are provided with detailed drawings and specifications. But even in the absence of exact plans, the client—even if you are the client and you are about to make something on speculation—has usually expressed certain ideas that already determine much about the piece. Those ideas may relate to the function it is to fulfill, the location it is to occupy, or the material out of which it is to be made, but few pieces spring into being from a total design vacuum.

The successful designer takes whatever is required and sensibly considers all the other factors that go into a piece's creation, orchestrating these elements into a cohesive whole. That responsibility is always there, if only because no two pieces of wood are identical, although in reality there are usually many decisions other than ones of material.

In the case of the television cabinet described here, the material, which was to be cherry, and the exterior dimensions and the interior arrangements were all clearly and exactly specified by the client. The design as given did not greatly appeal to me, and there did not appear to be much room for tasteful invention on my part, but I needed the work and reluctantly accepted the commission.

The specified outside dimensions were 5 feet wide, 3½ feet high, and 2½ feet deep. This created no particular feeling either way, but what did immediately concern me was that there was to be no base to this cabinet, no pediment, no moulding, and no ornament of any kind. It was to sit directly on the floor and, seen from the front, to consist solely of two identical doors that would open onto two identical compartments, one for a television and one for a stereo receiver. It was to be a perfectly rectangular volume with no subtle or flowing curves, no base to anchor it to the ground or elevate it with grace, no ornament to attract the eye, no moulding or shaping to delight one's sense of proportion, and no crowning pediment to give it direction: a simple geometric volume without even the opportunity to play with different woods, for it was to be made of solid cherry throughout (*Figure 1* shows the original dimensions).

*Figure 1 Given dimensions*

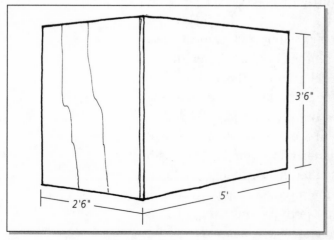

3'6"

2'6"    5'

**Material problems**—I chafed for a while at so many restrictions, but finally resigned myself to getting the job done as expeditiously as possible in order to move on to more interesting projects. I ordered the lumber and prepared to start.

When the wood arrived it was radically different from what I had expected. I had hoped to obtain wide boards of roughsawn cherry but none was available. Instead, I received several hundred feet of very narrow boards, almost all containing some white sapwood, and all cupped and warped. By the time I had dressed the material ready for working, instead of the four-quarter cherry I had envisaged at the start of the job, I was looking at a pile of narrow two-quarter-thick boards. The dramatic difference between what I had expected and what I actually had forced the first major design consideration.

I had thought I would build a rather bland cabinet, perhaps joining two or three quartersawn boards to obtain the necessary width of relatively homogenous material. Now I was faced with the necessity of matching numerous flatsawn boards.

Whatever the extra labor involved in obtaining the required width for the cabinet's carcase from a larger number of narrow boards, I was determined to save the widest boards for the panels of the front doors. These would constitute the most striking feature of the cabinet, and it was important that they appear as consistent as possible rather than being made up from several narrow boards, which would give them the character of randomly joined widths of cheap plywood doors. Since there was only one board available wide enough to form a front panel, the height of these panels was determined by dividing this board into four equal lengths. The board was about 10 inches wide and slightly less than 12 feet long. Bearing in mind the ¼-inch tongue that would be needed around each panel to fit it into its framing, this fixed each panel's finished visible surface at 9½ inches wide by 34 inches long.

The board had a little sapwood, but only on one side, and a small area of curl toward one end. The remainder of the board, being flatsawn, exhibited a pronounced "flame" pattern. I therefore cut the board into four lengths and arranged the pieces so that the two lengths from the curly end became the central panels, flanked by two flame-patterned outer panels. A little experimentation revealed which way around the panels looked best: the curly ones bookmatched and the outer panels with the tongues of the flames pointing upward. The effect was not very pronounced but definitely interesting and balanced. After checking that there was nothing glaringly unpleasant on the reverse side as arranged, I marked the pieces with chalk triangles to show front, top, and relative position (*Figure 2*).

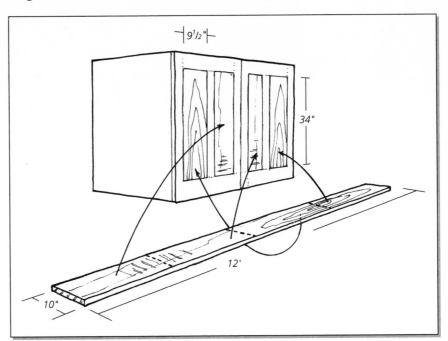

*Figure 2 The one wide board*

Another requirement that would prove problematical later was that the doors should open so that they might rest against the sides of the cabinet when the television or the stereo unit, which were to sit on slide-out shelves, was in use. This meant that the insides of the doors would frequently be in full view, unlike most cabinet doors, whose insides are only seen occasionally and momentarily. These, then, ought to be made with a little more care than usual, and it was necessary to pay attention to the pattern of the panels on the inside as well as on the outside, albeit only in pairs—since it would be impossible to see the insides of both doors at the same time. Because of the unequal distribution of sapwood and the positioning I had already determined, I now had a problem: One panel definitely cried out to be reversed end-for-end. But to do so would have ruined the front view. Play as I might with new arrangements, there seemed to be no way to make all panels look equally good. I was even unable to discover an acceptable compromise, something that is often forced by this kind of design. I finally took refuge in the fact that the only time the unhappy panel would be visible would be when something else—the television or the stereo—was the focus of attention.

Since the panels were together 40 inches wide, there remained only 20 inches to account for to produce the required finished width of 5 feet for the entire cabinet. Each door would need two stiles and a muntin, making a total of six vertical framing members. This suggested an average width for these pieces of a little less than 3½ inches. Having plenty of 6-inch-wide boards on hand, I didn't anticipate any stock selection problems and set about choosing boards for the carcase. I took the widest remaining boards for the top and sides so there would be the fewest number to join and the fewest choices to make regarding which edge looked best next to which edge—construction and aesthetics sharing equally in the design process.

Since every board was flatsawn and appeared to have been converted from very small trees, there was a lot of white sapwood and pronounced grain. Constructing a wide area of discrete homogeneity was not an option. In much cabinet construction, interest is focused on elements such as doors and panels, leaving the carcase as restrained as possible, usually by making it out of bland, straight-grained material typically produced by quartersawing. This carcase was not going to be polite enough to stay quietly in the background, so something had to be done to tame the wild excesses of each board's loud and obtrusive grain.

By aligning the boards so that sapwood abutted sapwood and heartwood abutted heartwood, I avoided much

*Figure 3
Arrangement of
boards comprising
carcase*

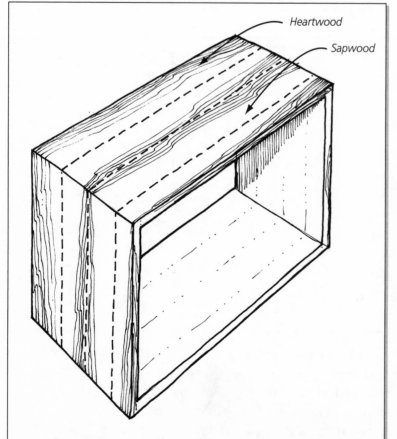

jarring of disparate grain and established a certain rhythm. The alternating light and dark was not exactly regular or even particularly well balanced, but the transition from heartwood to sapwood was more natural within each board because the line of demarcation at least followed the curve and sweep of the grain rather than being arbitrarily interrupted by the straight lines of the boards' joined edges (*Figure 3*).

I left the least-desirable boards for the bottom of the carcase. The underneath would never be seen and the top surface of the bottom would be hard to see beneath the sliding shelves and whatever was stored. Some of these boards were whole boards and some were ends of other boards I had chosen for the top and sides in an effort to achieve as much continuity as possible from side to top.

**Mechanical problems**—The problem concerning the way the doors were to open now made itself felt with what seemed like never-ending ramifications. The solution is typical of the way in which technical and aesthetic considerations must be sensitively juggled if satisfaction on all counts is to be achieved.

I had assumed that the doors would be hung inside the case rather than be face-mounted. The primary reason for this assumption lay in the fact that the cabinet was to have no base, and to guarantee easily operated doors on a possibly uneven floor or thick carpet some space should be left beneath the doors. This in turn meant that the front edges of the carcase would be visible, making their appearance important. Sure enough, the omnipresent sapwood glared out at various points around the perimeter.

My first response was to face-mount the doors, thus hiding the front edge of the carcase, but this returned me to the problem of doors possibly scraping an uneven floor or a thick carpet. My second idea was to set the doors back ¼ inch all around. But then where would the hinges be mounted? In fact, what *about* the hinges? Had the doors been set within the case as was the original assumption, what kind of hinges would have allowed the doors to open a full 270°, out and around the edge of the cabinet? Invisible hinges, Soss™-type hinges, and European-style hinges open a maximum of somewhat more than 180° but less than the required 270°. Knife hinges might be found that allowed the necessary

*Figure 4 Hingeing problems and solution*

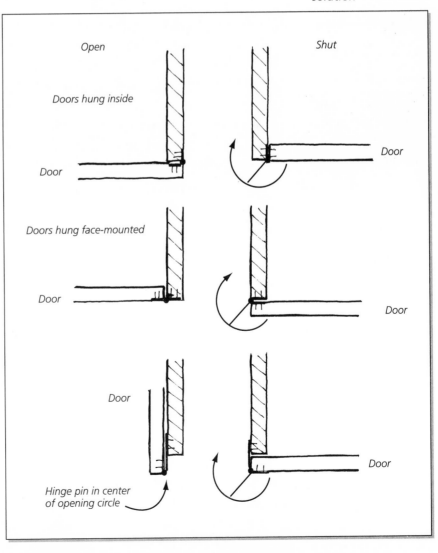

Open               Shut

Doors hung inside

Door            Door

Doors hung face-mounted

Door            Door

Door            Door

Hinge pin in center of opening circle

opening, but they would require the door to be hung within the frame—the very thing I was trying to avoid! The principle of leaf hinges became obvious: To open fully, the pivot point must be in the center of the circle around which the arc of the door's opening is described. Put more simply, the hinge pin must be at the extreme outside edge of door or frame. If door and frame are not flush, then the pin must be positioned in the right spot by means of variously bent leaves, similar to the offset hinges designed for face-mounted kitchen cabinet doors—which do not, however, open a full 270° (*Figure 4*).

Concern about the appearance of the front edge of the cabinet now became secondary to the problem of how to hang the doors so that they could be opened flat against the sides. The answer was to use not only surface-mounted hinges but surface-mounted doors as well. However, this still left the problem of finding a way to achieve flawless operation of the doors.

**Accepting defeat**—The juggling between construction and aesthetic consideration that plays such a large part in the design process may be described less charitably as compromise. In this case, the compromise involved accepting a small defeat with regard to the initial givens; my client agreed to a small base, abandoning the idea of having the cabinet rest directly on the floor.

The addition of a narrow, recessed base about 1 inch high not only allowed the doors to operate unimpeded but also improved the look of the piece enormously, demonstrating how often good form follows function. I now had a large rectangular volume that floated nicely just above floor level. The effect gave a certain delicate definition to the whole. It no longer appeared hunched, hulking uncompromisingly on the ground. This is, of course, largely a subjective point of view but it illustrates another aspect of design, namely that design is frequently a personal, individual matter. Certain absolute principles do exist that upon investigation are found to rest on demonstrable scientific or mathematical logic, but much good design is mere opinion—informed and felicitous, it is hoped, but a matter of taste just the same.

**Joinery as design**—The carcase could now be joined, its constituent boards in the manner described and then, when in the requisite sections, sides to top and bottom. Here was another opportunity: to use the actual joinery to enhance the design. Several structurally appropriate methods suggested themselves: mitered biscuit joints, locked rabbet joints, or dovetail joints. But dovetailing offered the most opportunity for interesting detail in an otherwise uninteresting area of casework, and despite the extra labor involved in joining what amounted to 10 linear feet of dovetailing, I decided it was worthwhile for the design's sake.

**Internal rhythms**—The cabinet was to consist of two equal compartments separated by a vertical divider. There was nothing to think about here. Had the doors been set within the case, a choice would have been possible between a recessed divider against which both doors would stop or a divider the front edge of which would finish flush with the front edge of the case, thereby forming an extra vertical member visible between the closed doors. But the only design choice that remained concerned the two compartments.

Each was to be fitted with a sliding shelf, one for a television and the other for a stereo receiver. The size of the two units dictated the approximate location of the shelves, but some leeway was possible. It could have been simply a matter of measuring off the height needed by each unit, allowing an inch or two for access, and positioning the shelves accordingly. But something more satisfying was possible. The cabinet measured 3½ feet high by 5 feet wide. The central vertical divider produced two vertical rectangles, each closely approximating a golden rectangle (in which the ratio of height to width is approximately 5:3)—a nicely balanced proportion producing compartments neither too narrow nor too wide. By positioning the shelves so that one was as far from the floor of the cabinet as the other was from the cabinet's ceiling, the feeling of comfortable balance was maintained, albeit asymmetrically (*Figure 5*).

This decision led to another idea. The left compartment was to hold the tele-

vision and was the one where the shelf was lower. The right compartment was to have the higher shelf for the stereo unit, thus leaving the lower area empty. This seemed not only a little uncomfortable but also somewhat inefficient because the space was really too high for the storage of things usual to such a cabinet, namely record albums, compact discs, videocassettes, and other audiovisual paraphernalia. An additional shelf was needed, not one that could slide in and out but one that could be raised and lowered. Here was something added to the design, something not originally called for in the plans but dictated by constant sensitivity to both form and function.

**Outside appearances—** To return to the doors— forming the entire front of the cabinet, they comprised the main design event—it was necessary to proportion

*Figure 5 Internal division into golden rectangles*

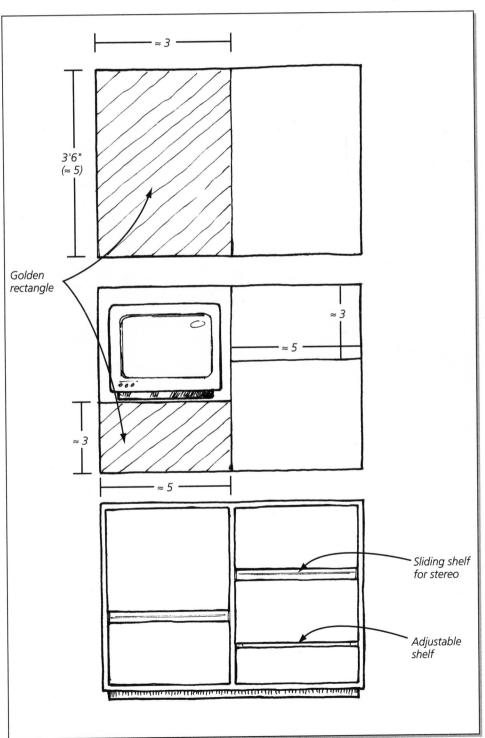

the framing as elegantly as possible. The mass of the cabinet as seen from directly in front presented a large and somewhat squat bulk. One way to overcome this oppressiveness would be to emphasize the verticality suggested by the four tall panels already cut. Accordingly, instead of making the bottom rail the widest member, as is usually done to provide a feeling of weight and groundedness (something this cabinet was not lacking), I made it the same width as the stiles.

The top rail, which is commonly the same width as the stiles, especially when these are narrower than the bottom rail, was made ½ inch narrower. Thus the framing was equal all the way around until it came to the top, where it was narrower. This produced a feeling a lightness. I further emphasized this top-lightness by making the central muntin of both doors the same width as the top rail. The muntin and the top rail gave the impression of being pushed upwards and outwards, and out of the surrounding, heavier frame.

By making the difference in width between the stiles and the muntins a mere ½ inch, I had tended to equalize all the vertical elements, further enhancing the dominant feeling of verticality. That the horizontal elements—the top and bottom rails—were decidedly insignificant by virtue of the fact that they were nowhere wider than any of the vertical members underlined the verticality even more.

The point where the two doors met produced, of course, double stiles. Their combined width nearly equaled the width of a panel, and in order to reduce this central weightiness I designed a pair of narrow, vertical handles, one for each stile. These formed a focus in the vast expanse of the flat front, and also pointed upward (*Figure 6*).

One last effect designed to aid in the general upward movement was the finishing of the sides of the panels with a ¼-inch bead. This was both functional and decorative. Functionally, the bead and its quirk disguise the gap that may appear between panel and frame should the panel shrink with seasonal dryness. Deco-

*Figure 6 Proportions
of frame members*

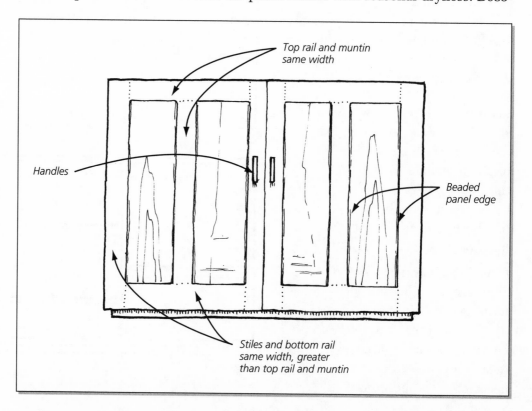

ratively, it formed the only motif in an otherwise plain geometric shape, defined only subtly by the proportions of the flush framing and paneling.

**Finishing touches**—The sliding shelves were to be side-hung on sliders screwed to stiffening pieces fixed to the bottom of the shelves. A face piece, the top of which was level with the top surface of the shelf, was fixed across the front, providing a way to pull out the shelf and at the same time hide the sliders. The width of these pieces was determined by the width of the shelves. Their height was determined by the necessity of providing at least enough wood to cover the front of the shelf and the stiffeners with their attached sliders (*Figure 7*). This resulted in a substantial front that called out for some shaping or relief. Relieving the bottom at the center produced a nice line but defeated the purpose of having somewhere to grab in order to pull out the shelf. The solution was to run a ¼-inch bead across the front, about two-thirds of the way up. This lightened the heavy effect of the plain front and united the inside of the cabinet with the outside by repeating the only decorative motif, the beading that ran up and down the sides of the panels. The fact that the beadings on the inside and outside ran perpendicular to each other emphasized the difference between the closed cabinet as an anonymous volume and the inside as a utilitarian space.

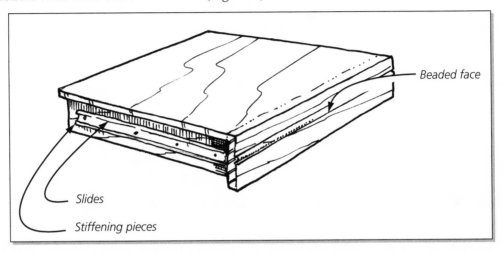

Beaded face

Slides

Stiffening pieces

*Figure 7 Sliding shelf*

The final result possessed infinitely more appeal than did the original design, although the specifications had been followed almost exactly. What made the difference was the attention to detail and a continuous awareness of a variety of design opportunities, elements that should be part of every project.

# CUTTING LIST

**Carcase:**

| | | |
|---|---|---|
| 1 top | .................................... | .60″ x 30″ x 1″ |
| 2 sides | ................................... | .42″ x 30″ x 1″ |
| 1 bottom | ................................. | .60″ x 32″ x 1″ |
| 1 partition | .............................. | .41″ x 32″ x 1″ |
| 1 back | ................................... | .60″ x 42″ x ¼″ |

(luan plywood)

**Base:**

| | | |
|---|---|---|
| 1 front | ................................... | .58″ x 1″ x 1″ |
| 2 sides | ................................... | .29″ x 1″ x 1″ |
| 1 back | ................................... | .58″ x 1″ x 1″ |

**Shelves:**

| | | |
|---|---|---|
| 2 shelves | ................................ | .28¼″ x 28″ x 1″ |
| 4 stiffeners | ............................. | .28″ x 4″ x 1″ |
| 2 fronts | .................................. | .28¼″ x 5″ x 1″ |

**Doors:**

| | | |
|---|---|---|
| 4 panels | ................................. | .35″ x 10″ x 1″ |
| 4 stiles | .................................. | .42″ x 3½″ x 1″ |
| 2 muntins | ............................... | .35″ x 4¼″ x 1″ |
| 2 top rails | .............................. | .24″ x 3¼″ x 1″ |
| 2 bottom rails | .......................... | .24″ x 4¼″ x 1″ |
| 2 handles | ............................... | .4″ x 1″ x 1″ |

**Hardware:**

4 hinges
2 pair of sliders
2 bullet catches

# A thinking man's chest

*Working with what's available*

This chapter, which could also be subtitled *Freedom from the cutting list,* addresses one of the most common problems faced by woodworkers attempting to build published projects: how to proceed if the cutting list for that particular project cannot be duplicated.

I have made many chests over the years, starting with simple toolboxes and storage containers, progressing all the way to elaborate pieces with moving parts. The construction techniques have ranged from basic six-board chests with rabbeted corners to frame-and-panel designs held together with a variety of sophisticated dovetail joints. Similarly, the wood I have used includes common lumberyard material such as pine, fir, and even spruce, as well as more expensive and exotic materials ranging from oak and walnut to amaranth and angiko.

Building repeated examples of the same type of piece is enormously instructive. Each variation has its own problems, the solutions to which make subsequent problems easier to solve. But you won't learn much if having figured something out you repeat the procedure blindly or, even worse, unthinkingly follow someone else's instructions and someone else's cutting list. It is better to keep an open mind so that even when repeating a design you remain alive to the possibility of doing something better here, something faster there, and maybe even changing an aspect of the design. This may not only produce a better-constructed piece, from both the structural as well as the procedural standpoint, but also can enrich the woodworking experience.

**An American original**—The design and fabrication of the "thinking man's chest" are straightforward. Apart from the carving, this chest is identical to one built toward the end of the nineteenth century, and which has been in my family for years. The original—still bearing traces of the original green milk-paint—had long impressed me with the rightness of its proportions. The construction seemed simple enough, and the fact that it had lasted so long was proof of the soundness of the design. My original intention was simply to make a companion copy, changing neither proportions, dimensions, nor construction techniques (*Figure 8*). But when the piece was finished, I had done more than simply copy someone else's design; I had gained a deeper appreciation of a chest considerably more sophisticated than what had been first apparent, and had learned invaluable lessons for constructing subsequent pieces.

**The material**—Although painted on the outside, it was easy to identify the material of the original as pine by looking closely at slightly damaged sections of

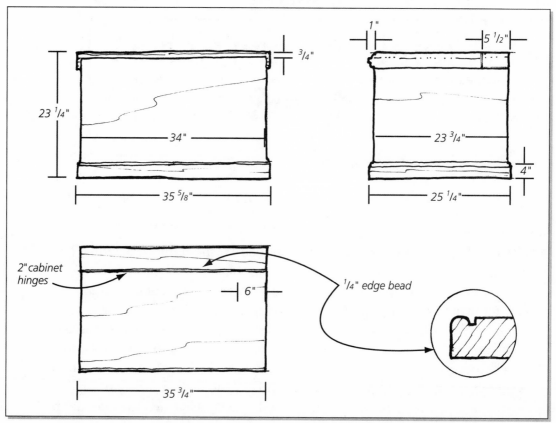

*Figure 8 Chest dimensions*

moulding and examining the dusty and discolored interior. But using the same species was as close as I was going to get. The original was clear pine, now much too expensive for the budget I had in mind for this project. Moreover, the front, back, and top were made from single boards. It is virtually impossible to find pine boards today wider than 16 inches, and so bang went my original idea of an authentic copy, correct to the last detail.

It is at this point, right at the beginning of a project, that many people will give up and look for something else to make, something for which they can find the exact material indicated in the cutting list. But unless you are out to make an absolutely authentic reproduction, there are often many alternatives. Your basic intention will determine the course you take. In this case I was endeavoring to follow the original builder's intent as well as my own. There were enough inconsistencies and small details to make it apparent that this was a handmade piece rather than the product of a factory, so it was fair to assume that the original builder had used what was most efficiently at hand. If this builder (let's call him Silas, for convenience) had believed that single-width boards were absolutely necessary, he would have used them on all four sides or not made the chest at all. But the existence of the chest suggests that Silas compromised and used whatever was easiest and best suited to the job from whatever was available.

I am guessing that he compromised because the underlying design here is that of the so-called "six-board chest" (see chapter 3). Often made from a single board, the sides, top, and bottom were simply cut to length, each part already being of the desired width, and were then joined to create a container with the minimum of fuss. This is both fast and structurally sound. Since the sides are all joined with the grain running in the same direction, any expansion or contraction takes place equally all the way around and consequently is usually unnoticeable. The top, being fixed only at the hinged edge and being given a 1-inch overhang at the front, is also free to move without any dimensional change being too apparent. Only the bottom is potentially troublesome, but, being hidden, does not present too large a problem.

Silas apparently did not have enough sufficiently wide stuff at hand to be able to get all six pieces from a single length, as would have been the ideal procedure, but undeterred, he did the best he could with what he had and used wide boards where they would work to best advantage. Similarly, not having anything wider than nominal 12-inch boards at my disposal, and clear stuff not being affordable, I did the best I could, making up the requisite width by piecing together narrower boards.

Far from regarding the inability to proceed along ideal lines with dismay and abandoning the project, both Silas and I achieved sufficient length of stuff capable of being finished to the required width of 22½ inches, and carried on. Moreover, my open-mindedness had provided me with advantages unavailable to Silas. He, no doubt, felt constrained by the need to take advantage of the economies of time that using wide boards made possible, while I was able to regard the use of scraps and smaller pieces as a necessary virtue, and to enjoy the patterning possibilities that result from using several pieces to make a single board.

**Carcase construction**—Another economic and aesthetic disadvantage of slavishly following the cutting list or abandoning the project if this is not possible deserves mention here. Simply providing oneself with the necessary parts as specified in the list without regarding them as a whole will hardly ever produce happy results. It would be far better to saw all six parts of the chest from two 16-foot lengths of 1-by-12 (a standard dimension available in most lumberyards), as shown in *Figure 8*, thereby allowing the grain to run harmoniously around the entire chest. But whether you possess sufficiently wide or long material to obtain the six parts shown in *Figure 9* to the measurements given in the cutting list by simply sawing the requisite parts to length or you have to piece together various odd sections, do so with an eye to how *all* parts will eventually join.

*Figure 9 Joining two boards to produce the six parts of a six-board chest*

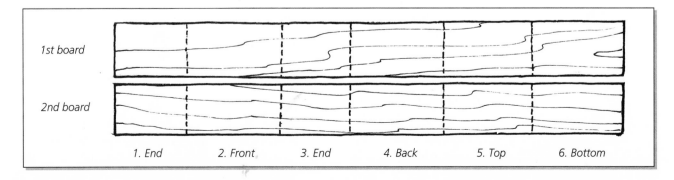

| 1st board | | | | | | |
| 2nd board | | | | | | |
| | 1. End | 2. Front | 3. End | 4. Back | 5. Top | 6. Bottom |

Each part can be pieced together with a simple butt joint, doweled together, splined, tongue-and-grooved, or even biscuit-joined. All these methods are illustrated at *Figure 10*.

Plain butt joints require that the edges to be joined be absolutely flat and true, and it is perhaps easier to accomplish this if you are working with shorter rather than longer lengths. For this reason, even if you start with two 16-foot-long

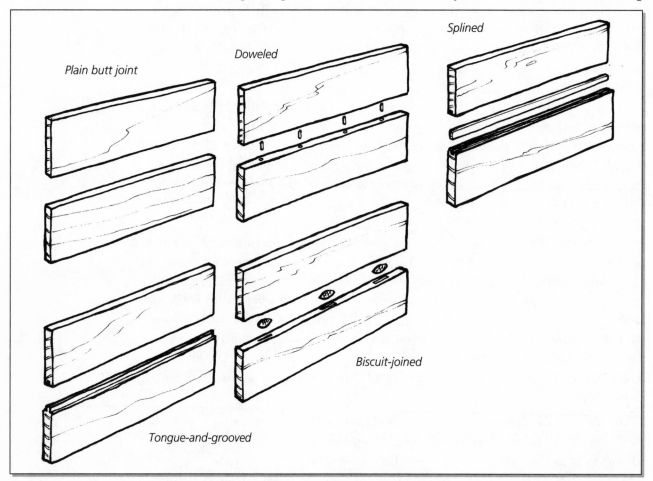

*Figure 10 Various ways to join boards*

boards (*Figure 9*), it might be better to saw out the parts first, being very careful to mark everything so the top of the front gets joined to the bottom of the front, and so on, and the order of the parts around the chest is not confused.

If you decide to use dowels or biscuits, make sure that they do not coincide with corners or you will be in for an unpleasant surprise when the sections are sawed apart.

I prefer to produce a flat face, then square as many edges as will have to be joined to achieve the needed width, and only then address the problem of thickness. If you have started with pre-thicknessed material such as 1-by-12 dressed stuff from the lumberyard, and work very carefully, nothing more than a light finishing on both surfaces will be needed.

The cutting list specifies 1-inch by 12-inch, 1-inch by 4-inch, and 1-inch by 6-inch material, and gives the finished thickness as ¾ inch. Dressed 1-inch material is usually close to an exact ¾ inch, so if all your material is bought at the same time, it should all match even if it is not, in fact, exactly ¾ inch. Silas's chest is made of stuff that is closer to 1 inch thick; the chest I made is a fraction thicker than ¾ inch; the cutting list specifies an exact ¾ inch; and I have just said that stuff somewhat thinner than ¾ inch would be fine—so what does all this mean? It means that once again it is the intention rather than exact duplication that is important. The intention is to produce a chest with certain given outside dimensions, that can be constructed in a sound manner.

A little forethought is necessary before deviating from any given measurement, but only enough to ensure that joints can still be cut as specified or in such a way that their structural integrity is preserved, and that any hardware such as hinges and handles will still fit where planned. While many projects may start from some absolute given, such as the need to build something to fit a particular space exactly, it is usually possible to exercise considerable discretion when interpreting cutting-list dimensions. It is true that a change in one part can often domino throughout the rest of the piece, and after thinking the effect through you may discover that at the very end of the chain you run up against another immutability, but more often, merely contemplating a change will bring other possibilities and improvements to light. People who build kitchen cabinets and spacecraft may have to stick to rigid specifications, but the making of freestanding furniture is a less exact science. An open mind can produce serendipitous improvements. It is in the nature of the material itself to surprise you, quite apart from unexpected errors that may force adaptation on the fly, since no two pieces of wood are exactly alike.

The corners of the original carcase are simply rabbeted, glued, and nailed. This is a relatively unsophisticated way of constructing a carcase but perfectly adequate if done well. I describe the process here, explaining a few subtleties, but there is no objection to other methods if you have a good enough reason. A good enough reason can be almost anything from a structural need—the intention to carry an extremely heavy load, for example—to a decorative impulse, such as the desire to show off Bermuda dovetails or some other unusual joinery. Or it could be simply the inspiration to indulge in some tricky technique for the pure pleasure of exercising your woodworking skills. Silas, no doubt, was only concerned with getting the job done in the most workmanlike fashion. My original impulse was to fulfill my need for a chest with something whose overall proportions appealed to me. Someone else may be trying to satisfy other demands. The method adopted will depend on the intention.

**Rabbeting**—The dimensions of the rabbets are shown in *Figure 11*. Remember that these assume stuff of a ¾-inch thickness. Obviously, the width of the rabbet should equal the actual thickness of the piece it is receiving, although a hair wider is useful if you plan on planing the endgrain of the rabbet flush with the surface of the sides after glue-up; the depth of the rabbet is a function of providing the merest step for the ends to butt up against, and is not much affected by any change in the thickness of the stuff. It is true that a deeper rabbet will provide more of a shoulder and make it easier to keep everything square when gluing up, but since you will be using clamps during this operation (which are easily manipulated to achieve perfect squareness of the body), it is more important to leave as much thickness as possible at the bottom of the rabbet to hold the fasteners (whether these are nails or screws) that enter from the outside of the front and of the back.

So far as the walls are concerned, only the front and back are rabbeted, but to accommodate the floor of the chest you must rabbet the bottoms of all four sides. Since the floor is liable to shrink and expand against the grain of the end

*Figure 11 Rabbet
dimensions*

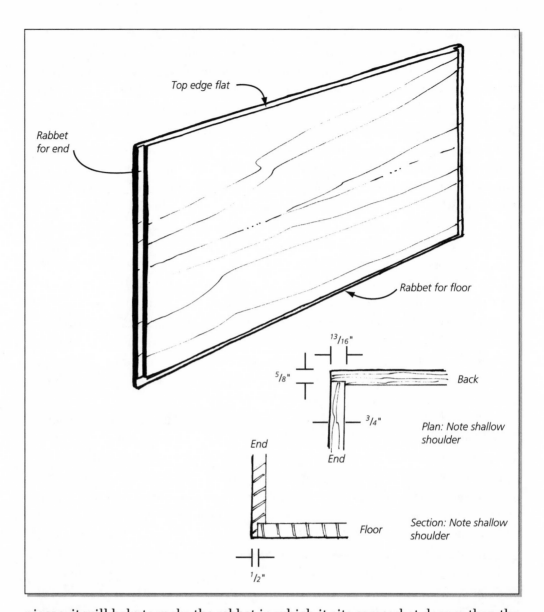

Top edge flat

Rabbet
for end

Rabbet for floor

13/16"

5/8"

Back

3/4"

*Plan: Note shallow
shoulder*

End

End

Floor

*Section: Note shallow
shoulder*

1/2"

pieces, it will help to make the rabbet in which it sits somewhat deeper than the rabbet provided in the front and back for the ends. This is still not an ideal solution. Silas didn't worry about this, probably for two reasons: First, his material was better seasoned than today's lumberyard pine, which although kiln-dried to national standards is by no means as stable as was his air-dried wood—the proof of which is the minimal amount of shrinkage that has occurred over the last ninety or more years—and in any event the piece was painted, which helps a lot in reducing changing moisture content (the reason for dimensional changes). Second, although the chest was built in a very workmanlike fashion—it is neatly executed and exhibits several caring touches that I describe later—I doubt that he was building for posterity, and his intentions were certainly not for woodworking perfection.

This raises another issue connected with slavishly following instructions rather than keeping the purpose of a piece clearly in mind. It is unlikely that we all share the same reasons for building any given piece. While technical information such as how to saw to a straight line or manipulate a router through a tricky maneuver may be vital, many other aspects, such as the exact depth or type of rabbet, may well be irrelevant.

Bearing this in mind, if your goal is cabinetmaking perfection, you might prefer to cut a rabbet in the floor in the form of a tongue, with a matching groove in the insides of the sides (*Figure 12*). This will allow the floor to expand and contract without conflicting with the ends. However, you will lose the extra support and strength that the fasteners used in the original would have provided. If securely nailed in place, the original floor runs the risk of splitting if it contracts,

or, even worse, of pushing the sides apart if it expands, but it gains substantial strength useful if the chest is to be carried around with heavy loads, and also serves to guarantee the rectilinearity of the bottom of the chest. Moreover, you may not be able to cut sufficiently deep grooves in the sides to accommodate all possible movement of the floating floor, and the floor might shrink so much that it drops out! There are ways, of course, to provide for these eventualities, such as raising the floor and fixing a substantial ledger beneath it, attached to the sides with slotted screws at the ends to support it, or even by making the floor a frame-and-panel construction, but this would all be inconsistent with the plain rabbet joints used on the sides—a bit like carpeting a cheap car with the finest Persian rug.

Nevertheless, if this is your intention, go ahead, but if, like Silas or myself, you simply need a sturdy and well-proportioned chest built as efficiently as possible, accept the compromise. The point is not to feel locked into the instructions, but to keep your own goals in mind.

**Gluing up**—However you may have prepared the parts of the carcase, the time will come when they must be assembled. Unless you have used some form of self-supporting joinery, such as dovetails or locking corner joints, you must prepare for this carefully. If possible, secure an additional pair of hands.

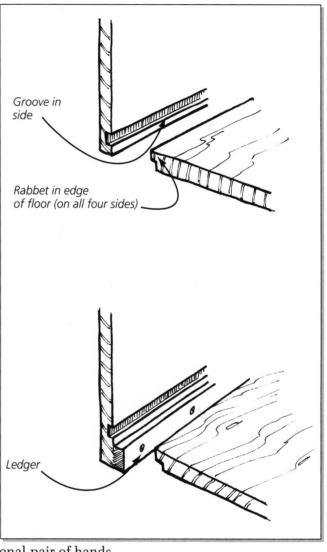

*Figure 12 Floating floor joinery*

The easiest method is to assemble the sides first, upside down, with glue in the rabbets and held together with just a couple of bar-clamps or pipe-clamps running from front to back. Before nailing or screwing, pop in the floor, because this will make the corners square (providing it has been cut out carefully and checked for squareness). Silas's chest was simply nailed with what are now regarded as rather handsome, period cut-nails. I chose to use countersunk screws and plug the holes. With a little planning, attractive patterns can be created by grouping the screws and using contrasting wood as plugs, but don't bother with this if you intend to paint the chest.

Even with the floor in place, it is a good idea to check the squareness of the top and adjust if necessary by a little judicious repositioning of the clamps. Placing the clamps out of parallel with the sides will skew the box (or remove any skew). Be aware that if you tighten the clamps too much, especially when using pipe clamps, which can deflect out-of-straight under pressure, you will not be able to check squareness by placing a framing square on the corner because the sides may be bowed. A better method of checking squareness is to measure the diagonals across the top of the chest (*Figure 13*); they should be equal.

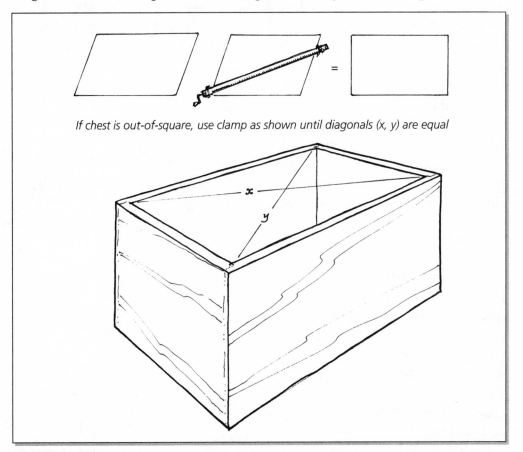

*If chest is out-of-square, use clamp as shown until diagonals (x, y) are equal*

*Figure 13 Method
of checking
rectilinearity*

**The plinth**—When the clamps have been removed, any excess glue cleaned up, and the endgrain of the rabbets planed as suggested earlier, it is time to make the plinth.

The structural purpose of the plinth is to protect the bottom of the chest and cover the nails holding the floor. Aesthetic considerations are more subtle. A plinth of a certain size can function adequately so far as structure is concerned but look poorly proportioned. To some extent this is subjective, and if you like the way the piece looks as made according to the cutting list, then follow these measurements. Otherwise, express yourself how you will, but do so in an informed way. To help you do this I give here detailed instructions on the hand method probably followed by Silas, since this is no longer the most common method.

The simplest form for plinths on chests this size is usually one about 4 inches high. It is usually finished with a moulded top edge, even if this moulding is nothing more than a simple chamfer. The reason is very practical: A moulded edge has less of an extreme arris and as such is less likely to be damaged or collect dust; even a simple chamfer will provide less of a shelf for dust than would a square-edged plinth.

Silas's plinth was finished with a common ovolo, the moulding profile often seen on wooden window sashes, and was undoubtedly made with a sash moulding plane. The same moulding is used for the front edge of the lid. These two facts suggest that our Silas was more a carpenter than a cabinetmaker; carpenters were likely to make windows rather than furniture, and consequently had less use for the fancier profiles favored by furnituremakers.

While the modern method might be to use a router or a shaper fitted with the appropriate bit, sash ovolo planes are by no means rare and often can be found at fleamarkets and in antiques shops for the same price as a good router bit. Their use is quiet, easy, and pleasant. If you use the modern tool, nothing more is required than to choose an appropriate bit and take care to avoid any chattering, burning, or routing of knotty material. But if the nicer feel of a hand-planed moulding is decided upon, the following points must be borne in mind: First, since the moulding plane is a plane like all other planes, you should try to plane with the grain. And since you are planing on an arris, you must take into account the grain not only on the face of the wood but on its edge as well. Second, a moulding plane is commonly used in the reverse direction from a bench plane. That is, you do not start at the back end of the wood and plane towards the front, but rather you must begin at the far end of the wood and, while still planing in a forward direction, gradually work your way backwards, starting each stroke closer to the near end until the entire length has been worked.

It is also advisable to prepare a length of moulding rather longer than the actual length required because you will lose a certain amount of the length when cutting miters for the corners, and because it is difficult to plane the extreme ends of a piece to an exact shape.

Clean up the moulding with a small rabbet plane or a wooden rubber cut to shape. Cut the pieces to length using a miter box, holding the back of the miter against the back of the box to avoid a ragged edge at the front of the miter. Remember that the measurement you take along the bottom edge of the chest is the *inside* measurement of the plinth piece, not the measurement from the end of one miter to the end of the other.

Be sure to cut on the waste side of the line when sawing the miters. Trim down to the line for a perfect fit using a block plane and a donkey's-ear miter shooting board. This is an easy piece of shop equipment to make, similar to a bench hook, and guarantees exact miters, especially when they are tall in relation to their width (*Figure 14*).

Make the front piece first and fix it with finishing nails. In this way, if the chest is still slightly out of square, you will be able to adjust the side miters to fit, which is an easier business than vice-versa.

**The lid**—All that remains is the lid, which comprises three parts: the hinge jamb, the top, and the cleats. The hinge jamb is a simple idea not often seen but very useful. It provides an additional guarantee of squareness for the back and sides of the chest, and solves the problem all too often encountered with chest lids that are hinged

*Figure 14 Using donkey's ear shooting board to trim plinth miters*

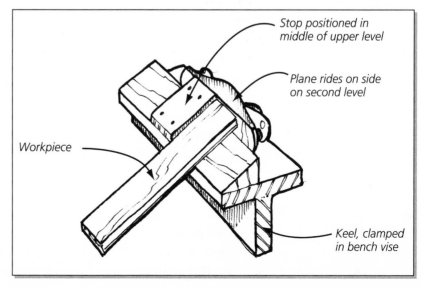

Stop positioned in middle of upper level

Plane rides on side on second level

Workpiece

Keel, clamped in bench vise

directly to the back of the chest, whereby the weight of a carelessly opened lid can pull it off the hinges.

It is nailed directly to the top of the back and the ends. Its front edge is finished with a ¼-inch bead, which softens the edge and turns the unavoidable gap between the lid and hinge jamb into a nice, moulded feature. The back is made flush with the back of the chest, but the sides extend past the ends sufficiently to accommodate short pieces continuing the line of the cleats that will be fixed at the under edges of the top. Note that a little clearance will be necessary between the inside edges of the cleats and the ends of the chest; you should not fix their mates under the hinge jamb close against the sides of the ends of the chest, but leave a similar gap of no more than ⅛ inch.

Once again, the only vital part of the above from a structural standpoint is the existence of the jamb itself. Even its exact width is not an absolute; as given, it reflects the standard width of a nominal 1-by-6 as sold in today's lumberyards. All other details can be changed or even omitted. As described, they are witness to Silas's sensitivity to a level of work consistent with an age that produced joinery and millwork to a standard considerably higher than much of today's. But there are other ways to achieve the same effects, such as making the continuation of the end cleats from ¾-inch stock and being able thereby to fix them tightly against the side of the chest while still having their outside face be flush with that of the ¾-inch-thick cleats. There is also no reason why the front edge of the lid should not be finished with a common thumbnail moulding. Do not take for granted the unalterability of the cutting list.

The lid itself in its simplest form is one piece, deep enough to span the distance from the front of the hinge jamb to a point 1 inch past the front of the chest, and wide enough to accommodate 1-by-2 cleats at each side.

The overhang at the front serves the purpose of providing somewhere to lift the lid easily and also to disguise any expansion or contraction. Its exact measurement is a matter of taste and how the moulding looks in profile. Silas's ovolo looks best if its top fillet is more or less in line with the outside face of the front (*Figure 15*). A more usual moulding such as the thumbnail variety might happily protrude a little more; a chamfer might require less of a protrusion. Before you decide, consider the given measurements and any alternatives that come to mind.

The cleats not only help keep Silas's single-board top flat—which might not be so necessary if the top were made from a number of pieces whose orientation with respect to the center of the tree from which they were cut was alternated—

*Figure 15  Lid front profiles*

but also provide a measure of airtightness and dust protection when the lid is closed, and would be useful even if the top were made in a manner that required no help to ensure flatness.

The profile of the front ends of the cleats echoes the profile of the moulding

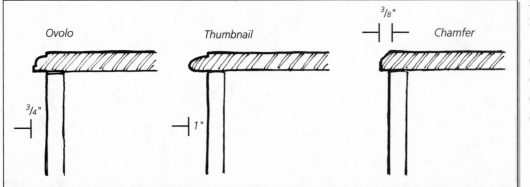

formed on the front edge of the top—another sensitive detail adding to the harmony of the piece.

**Last details**—Handles fixed to the ends are virtually indispensable if the chest is to be moved easily, but the carving is entirely optional. I love simple chip carving in pine, and find it especially useful for diverting attention from knots. Of course, the pieces that constitute the various parts of my chest were assembled with an eye as to how best to arrange these unavoidable features of number one grade material (clear pine is graded as "clear"; a few small, tight knots constitute grade 1, larger knots constitute grade 2, and so on), and in turn played a part in dictating the type and location of carving used, since I had chosen not to paint my chest like Silas's but to finish it with a coat of linseed oil.

This kind of decision has to be unique to each piece, and while it may be necessary at first to follow instructions in order to learn the various processes and understand their rationale, it is a final example of the initiative we must practice if we are to be anything more than kit assemblers.

## CUTTING LIST

**Carcase:**

1 front . . . . . . . . . . . . . . . . . . . . . . . . . . . . . . .34″ x 22½″ x ¾″

1 back . . . . . . . . . . . . . . . . . . . . . . . . . . . . . . .34″ x 22½″ x ¾″

2 ends . . . . . . . . . . . . . . . . . . . . . . . . . . . . . .22½″ x 22½″ x ¾″

(assumes ⅛-inch-deep rabbet in front and back)

1 floor . . . . . . . . . . . . . . . . . . . . . . . . . . . . . .33″ x 22¾″ x ¾″

(assumes ¼-inch-deep rabbet in sides)

**Plinth:**

1 front . . . . . . . . . . . . . . . . . . . . . . . . . . . . . .35⅝″ x 4″ x ¾″

1 back . . . . . . . . . . . . . . . . . . . . . . . . . . . . . . .35⅝″ x 4″ x ¾″

2 sides . . . . . . . . . . . . . . . . . . . . . . . . . . . . . .25¼″ x 4″ x ¾″

**Lid:**

1 lid . . . . . . . . . . . . . . . . . . . . . . . . . . . . . . . .35¾″ x 19¼″ x ¾″

1 lid jamb . . . . . . . . . . . . . . . . . . . . . . . . . . . .35¾″ x 5½″ x ¾″

2 cleats . . . . . . . . . . . . . . . . . . . . . . . . . . . . . .19¼″ x 1½″ x ¾″

2 lid jamb cleats . . . . . . . . . . . . . . . . . . . . . .5½″ x 1½″ x ¾″

*Note: All the above parts may be made from standard number one nominal ¾-inch pine.*

**Hardware:**

1 pair chest handles

1 pair of 2-inch cabinet hinges

# Six-board chest

*Underlying construction principles*

The six-board chest is included as an example of the effect that construction principles can have on the design of any given piece. Despite the admonition in the introduction concerning Ruhlman's demands that design not be limited by craftsmanship, it is a fact that just as form very often follows function, so it also can follow the dictates and requirements of construction. This is especially true of pieces built in a traditional manner. The very term "traditional" implies a construction that has proved its worth as a tried-and-true method. Had the construction been faulty or wanting, it would not have survived to be perpetuated time after time and so become "traditional."

Moreover, and especially to the point under discussion in this book, the design element in such traditional pieces must also have been successful. It is hard to think of any traditional pieces or styles that although constructionally sound are inherently unsuccessful as designs, whether this be a measure of beauty, utility, or appropriate use of available materials. Design includes all these things.

Considering only the aesthetic angle, we may have personal opinions regarding certain styles. Chippendale may be more to one person's taste than is Art Nouveau, but had either style been fundamentally unsuccessful from a design standpoint, it would not have survived long enough to become traditional—of any period. Equally true is that had the construction been faulty, the design would not have been successful. An examination of traditional pieces is thus useful for discovering successful design principles, one important clue to which is traditional construction.

If, therefore, we understand the construction of a traditional piece, we are then bound to understand part of its success as a design. The six-board chest is a clear example of this, the more so because of its simplicity. Its design can be described, explained, and justified in terms of its construction. Its construction, while straightforward, is admirably to the point. The way the six boards are chosen and prepared, the joinery involved for the construction of the carcase, the way the bottom and top are made all contribute unerringly to a sound design. On an even deeper level, the very design of the dovetails is largely a function of good construction. The slope of the tail is dictated by the need to produce a joint that will withstand certain pressures and tensions. The way this slope may be altered to take into account the effect of different densities of wood—a soft wood, for example, requiring a greater slope than does a hard wood—is a perfect example of form following construction.

This chapter describes the construction of a generic six-board chest, and consequently no dimensions are given and no cutting list is included. The construction is explained in more detail and somewhat differently than it was done in the previous chapter, but you should be aware that the different methods are interchangeable. The proportions should be adapted according to the material at hand and to whatever specific need you may have. As you make decisions concerning dimensions and techniques, remember what was said in chapters 1 and 2 about how the parts and the whole look.

A six-board chest is so-called because theoretically it can be made from six boards: two for the ends, one for the front, one for the back, one for the top, and one for the bottom. Boards wide enough to construct chests measuring 18 inches to 2 feet high are no longer as common as they once were, however, and to build a chest this size you will probably have to glue up two or more boards to produce the required width for each piece.

**Doweled edge joints**—A good way to start is to use regular "one-by" pine. As bought from a building supply or lumberyard, "one-by" pine actually measures closer to ¾ inch by whatever width you choose from the standard widths available, typically 4, 6, 8, 10, or 12 inches, and may be bought in lengths up to 16 feet long. Two boards of similar length joined together can be cut into the six boards required for a six-board chest, and if you cut out the six pieces as shown in *Figure 9* in chapter 2, the grain pattern will run nicely around the chest.

If you need to join boards to achieve a sufficient width, choose the face side of each board and plane perfectly true the edges that are to be joined. Place these two edges together, and mark the divisions for each of the six pieces so that you don't end up boring holes for the dowels that will join them at the places you will be sawing.

*Figure 16 Marking dowel positions*

Between the division lines make marks every 8 inches or so to indicate the position of the dowels. Square these marks across the true edges and then bisect these lines with a marking gauge (*Figure 16*).

Choose dowels and a matching drill bit or auger bit with a diameter no greater than half the thickness of the board. If you use a doweling jig, it will be easy to bore all the holes perfectly straight and to the same depth (½ inch to ¾ inch). If you don't have a doweling jig, wrap a piece of tape around the bit to act as a depth gauge,

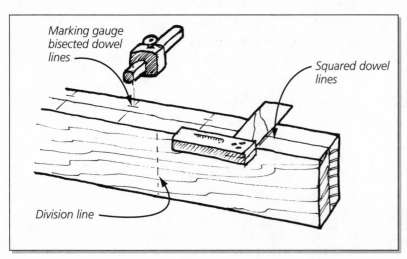

Marking gauge bisected dowel lines

Squared dowel lines

Division line

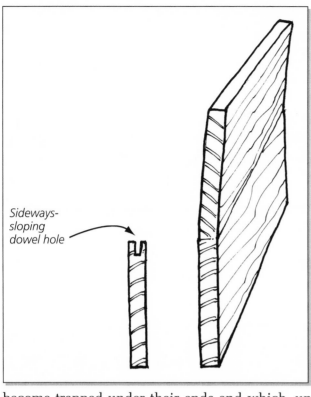

Sideways-sloping dowel hole

and take care to bore straight by standing at the end of the work and keeping the drill or brace in line with the work. If the hole slopes a little toward or away from the ends, this will only result in a certain amount of strain during assembly, whereas a hole that slopes to the side will cause the boards to be out-of-square (*Figure 17*).

Cut the dowels slightly shorter than the combined depth of two holes, and round their ends a little to make insertion easy. The dowels should be grooved to provide an escape channel for any glue that might

*Figure 17 Effect produced by misaligned dowel holes*

become trapped under their ends and which, under pressure, might cause the wood to split. The easiest way to groove dowels is by knocking them through a hole in a scrap piece that has a nail sticking into it (*Figure 18*). As an additional precaution, you can countersink the ends of the holes in the boards, but it is better workmanship not to apply more glue than is necessary in the first place.

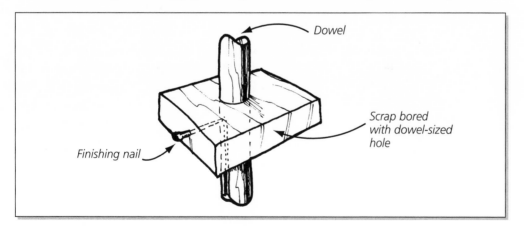

Dowel

Scrap bored with dowel-sized hole

Finishing nail

*Figure 18 Dowel grooving*

Glue the edge of one board, spreading the glue evenly and making sure that a little goes into each hole. Tap the dowels home with a mallet, similarly glue the edge of the second board, and then fit it over the doweled board. Clamp the boards together, using scraps to prevent the jaws of the clamps from denting the edges and alternating the clamps from side to side to keep the boards in the same plane, and wipe off any squeeze-out.

**Dovetail joinery**—When the glue has set, saw the board into the six pieces required for the chest. Remember to make the width of the chest slightly less than the width of the glued board so that the top will cover the chest (*Figure 19*).

Dovetail joinery provides the strongest corner joint. Although it may look complicated, if the proportions are understood, the execution is straightforward.

The joint consists of two parts: dovetails and pins. The dovetails are the pieces that look like doves' tails when viewed from the *face* of the wood. While it is possible to become confused by observing that the *ends* of the other part of the joint also look like doves' tails, note that these would, in fact, form reversed doves' tails when the joint is assembled; this part of the joint is called the pin (*Figure 20*).

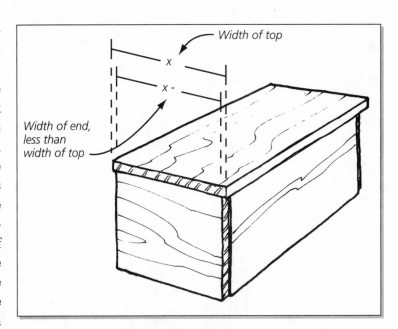

*Figure 19  Width of top relative to ends*

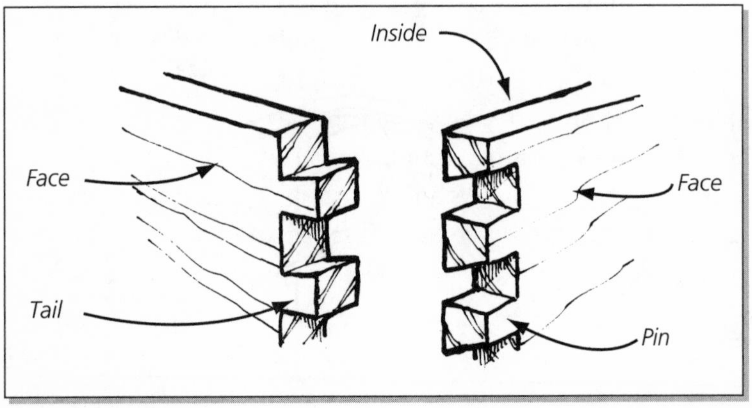

*Figure 20  Parts of a dovetail joint*

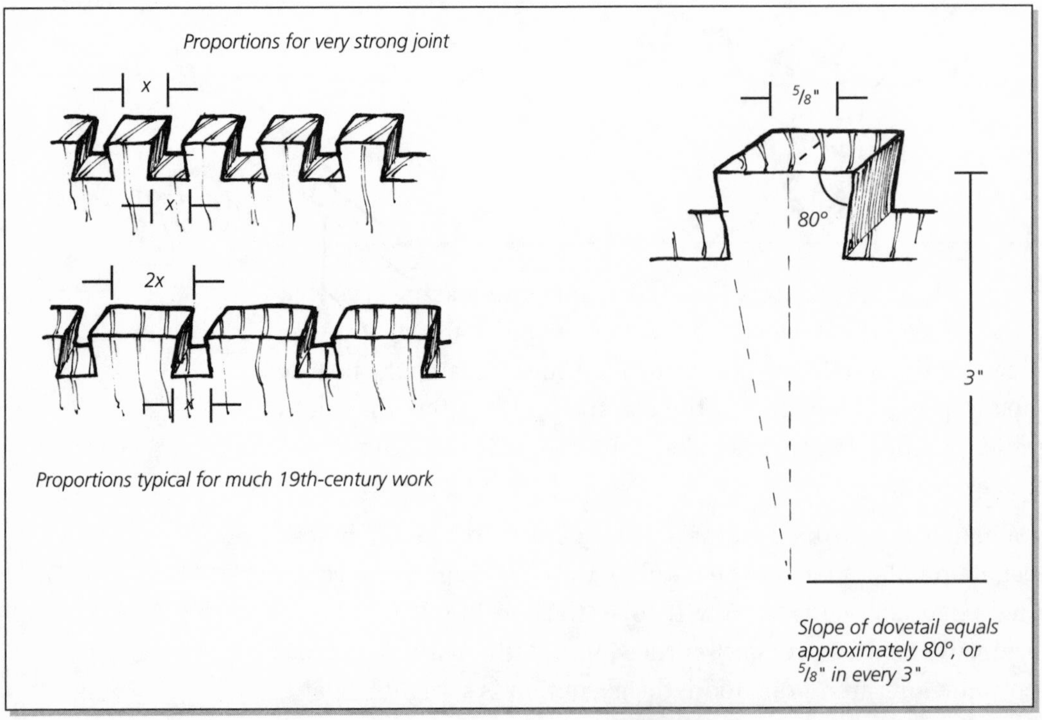

*Figure 21  Dovetail proportions*

The angle of the dovetails can be made somewhat steeper for hardwood, but a slope of 80° is fine for pine. This is most easily established by setting a bevel to open to ⅝ inch at a distance of 3 inches. For very strong joints, the distance between the dovetails should equal the ends of the dovetails, but for average work you may double the spacing and halve the cutting. In old work the widest part of the dovetails often measured slightly more than half the thickness of the material being used (*Figure 21*).

To begin, square off a line around all the ends at a distance equaling ⅟₁₆ inch greater than the thickness of the material. Having decided on the proportions to be used—and bearing in mind that the dovetails are cut on the side pieces of the chest, and

*Proportions for very strong joint*

*Proportions typical for much 19th-century work*

*Slope of dovetail equals approximately 80°, or ⅝" in every 3"*

that it is a half-dovetail that forms the top and bottom corners—lay out the dovetails on the ends of the side pieces using a bevel and a sharp knife (*Figure 22*).

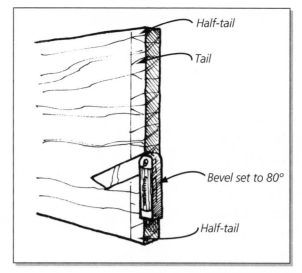

Using a dovetail saw, cut carefully on the waste side of the line marking the dovetails. Sawing two ends together saves time. Securing the pieces so that the cut can be made vertically helps accuracy.

Remove the waste by first sawing along the bottom of the dovetail with a coping saw and then paring to the line with a chisel, working from each side to avoid splitting out the wood (*Figure 23*).

Lay the finished dovetails over the ends of the front and back, and mark and saw out the pins (*Figure 24*). Take care not only to have previously marked which ends are to join (in order to preserve any continuity of grain around the chest), but also to remember when marking the pins

*Figure 22 Laying out dovetails on sides*

*Figure 23 Cutting dovetails*

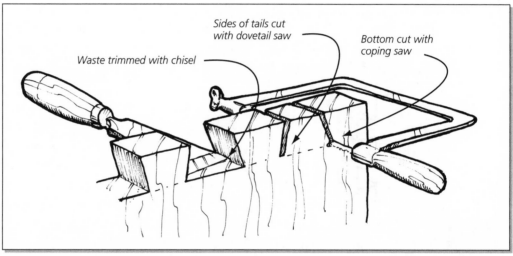

*Figure 24 Marking and sawing the pins*

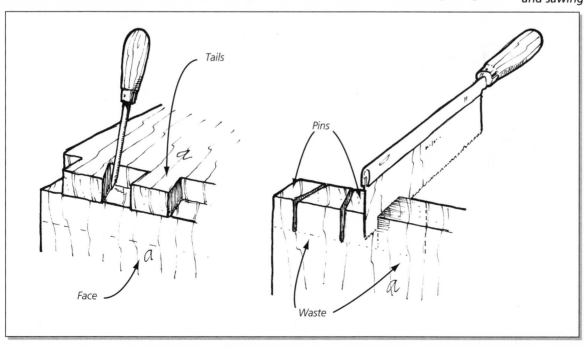

that it is the *narrow* part of the pins that must appear on the face of the work. Remove the waste between the pins as you did between the dovetails, and then bevel slightly the inside edges of the dovetails to ease assembly and lessen the chance of splitting anything. How well the joint goes together will depend on how accurately you have marked and cut the tails and pins; your first attempts may require a little paring. Work slowly and do not force the joint together. Properly formed, the joint should require only light taps with the mallet to assemble the two parts, using a length of scrap to protect the work.

When all four corners have been cut and tested for fit, glue and assemble. If you use metal clamps, place scrap pieces under the jaws to protect the wood and position them so that they do not interfere with any pins or tails. Be sure to keep the corners of the chest square. When the glue has dried, trim any projecting ends with a block plane, working in from the corners and ends to avoid splitting the edges.

*Figure 25 Stages in planing moulding*

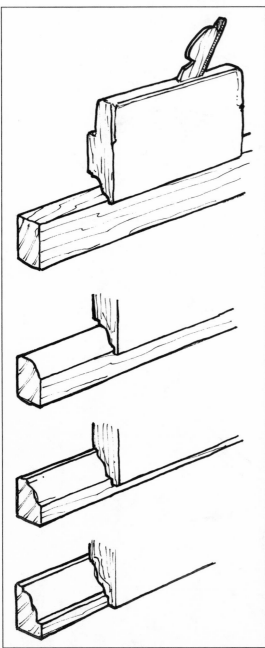

**The bottom and plinth**—Cut and plane the bottom piece to fit snugly within the four sides, and then nail it in place. This is stronger than nailing it from underneath, even though in time it may shrink a little as the wood dries. Gaps caused by such shrinking can be avoided by cutting a rabbet in the bottom of the front and back before assembly and setting the bottom in this rabbet; however, since many old chests were lined, this is rarely seen.

Make the plinth that covers the nail holes from a length of "one-by" material sufficient to run around the entire base, allowing for a little extra at each corner to accommodate the miters. The top edge can be moulded for appearance and to prevent splintering. A simple chamfer will suffice; something more elaborate can be made by using a moulding plane.

Since few moulding planes have capirons, it is best to plane with the grain. Since the moulding plane cuts on an arris, you should take into account the direction of the grain not only on the top of the piece but on the side as well. Remember also that unlike a bench plane, a moulding plane is started at the far end of the workpiece, each successive stroke being taken closer to the near end so that the plane runs into the profile already formed (*Figure 25*).

Cut the pieces to length using a miter box. Remember that the measurement you take along the bottom edge of the chest becomes the inside measurement of the plinth.

Proper use of the miter box involves holding the back edge of the workpiece against the back of the miter box to avoid forming a ragged edge at the front of the miter. Be sure to cut on the waste side of the line and trim down to this line for a perfect fit using a block plane in a donkey's-ear miter shooting board. This is a fairly easy piece of equipment to make and the only safe way to plane tall miters (see *Figure 14*, chapter 2).

Make the front piece of the plinth first and fix it with finishing nails. It is easier to adjust the side miters to fit those of the front piece than vice-versa. Finally, make and fit the rear piece.

**The lid**—Saw the piece for the lid somewhat longer than the chest to allow for the wood that will be lost when the ends are planed smooth, and because a small overhang is necessary to allow the lid moulding to clear the sides. Since most wood will inevitably shrink somewhat, especially pine, make the top ½ inch wider as well.

The lid moulding will help keep the lid flat, form a dust lip, and close the lid more effectively, and for appearance' sake should echo the plinth in form, although it may be smaller.

Mould, miter, and fit the pieces in the same manner as you did the plinth, but note that in order for the lid to open, no moulding is used at the rear of the lid!

You may hinge the lid in a variety of ways, including using surface-mounted decorative strap hinges, but the least-obtrusive method is to use plain butt-hinges mortised into the underside of the lid and the top edge of the chest back.

# Desk box

*The interplay of construction and function*

The desk box illustrates a similar force to that of construction on design as described in the previous chapter, namely that of function. "Form follows function" is repeated so often we tend to lose sight of its importance as one of the great pillars of wisdom upon which good design rests. Furniture is distinguished from other constructions by its need to fulfill a useful function—not merely an aesthetic or expressionistic function, but a truly utilitarian function. It must, for example, contain an object, support a person, or provide a work surface. If it has no other purpose than to delight the senses, it may be a work of art, a masterpiece, or a dazzling tour-de-force, but it is not truly furniture. Furniture must function. Function, therefore, is an indispensable part of furniture design that if ignored can result in the piece's failure no matter how beautiful or well constructed it may be.

Whatever else the desk box is, it is a functioning piece of furniture. Its functioning—the slope of its lid, which facilitates comfortable writing; the capaciousness of its interior; the division of its interior into separate spaces for convenient storage of items necessary for writing—is central to its design. To design a piece successfully requires, among other things, that it function adequately for the purpose for which it is designed. Although this may sound dangerously close to tautology, it is surprising how many so-called pieces of furniture are produced that fail miserably in their avowed purpose: chairs that collapse if anyone heavier than a child sits on them, tables that you can't get your legs underneath, boxes whose bottoms fall out when anything heavier than a telephone directory is carried in them. These failings may be the result of poor construction but they are also often the result of *inappropriate* construction. The butt joint used in the box's carcase may be well made and neatly executed but simply the wrong joint for the purpose.

Understanding all this, if we develop a design bearing in mind its function, we will necessarily include construction techniques that will exert their own

influence on the design.
The desk box must be of
a sufficient size to hold
at least average sheets of
writing paper. This is
not very large, so a top
may be made that con-
sists of a single plane. A
larger area might require
additional construction
techniques such as frame-
and-paneling, to pro-
vide stability. Since
additionally the desk
box is by its very nature
more special than a box
designed, for example,
to hold potatoes, it makes
sense to use a better
material than common-
place pine or even plywood. Both of these could be used with constructional suc-

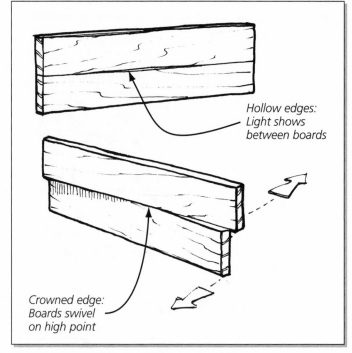

*Hollow edges:
Light shows
between boards*

*Crowned edge:
Boards swivel
on high point*

*Figure 26  Testing for straightness*

cess but they would less successfully result in
something special or beautiful. These functions
are also important.

**Joinery**—Unlike pine, which was used for the two
previous pieces, walnut, although readily available, is not always available in standard sizes.
Length probably won't be a problem, but it's possible that the lid and the bottom will have to be
made from several pieces. It may help to obtain
pieces long enough so that, when joined together
to form the required width, they can be sawed in
half to make the lid and the bottom.

When joining lengths, arrange the pieces so
that the grain either blends or contrasts nicely. Use

*Amount of misalignment*

*Joint is tight, but –*

*Gap shows under straightedge*

*Figure 27  Testing
joint for squareness*

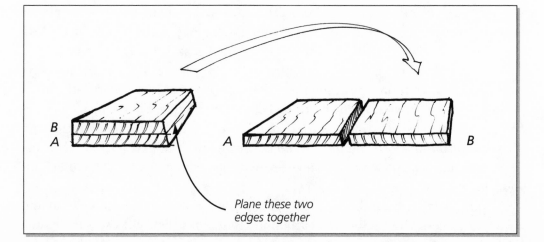

*Figure 28  Joining
two boards into
same plane*

*B*
*A*

*A*

*B*

*Plane these two
edges together*

the occasional blond areas characteristic of walnut to good effect, but try also to alternate the grain from piece to piece, since this counteracts any tendency to warp excessively.

If you do have to join pieces to achieve the required width, all that is required here is a plain edge- or butt joint. Since there is no inherent mechanical strength in such a joint, it is very important to plane the edges as perfectly as possible.

Test for the straightness of the edges by placing one board on top of the other. If light shows between the joint, the edges are hollow; if the top board swivels, the edges are rounded (*Figure 26*).

If the joint is tight along its length, test to see that the boards lie in the same plane by holding a straightedge against them (*Figure 27*). Misalignment may be corrected by planing the offending edge square or by planing both edges at once so that any out-of-squareness will be the same on both edges and will be canceled out when the boards are assembled (*Figure 28*).

When all edges match, glue and clamp them. For short lengths, one clamp may suffice; if more are used, alternate them. But if the joints fit well, merely rubbing the edges together so that the ends and faces align will be enough. Wipe away any excess glue and stand the boards to one side to dry, preferably overnight.

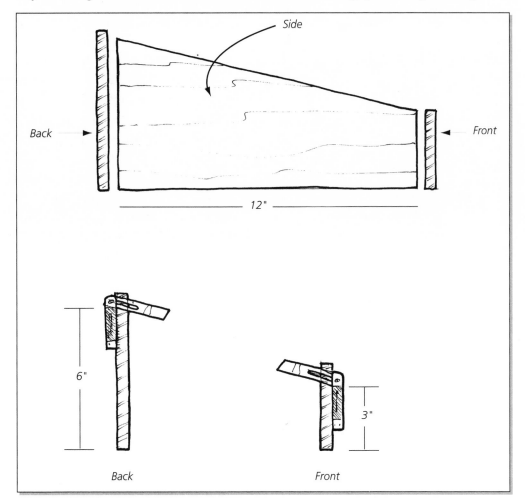

*Figure 29 Side dimensions and layout of front and back*

Cut the sides first, to the dimensions shown in *Figure 29*. Then cut the front and back to the exact length but 1 inch greater than the given width to allow for beveling later.

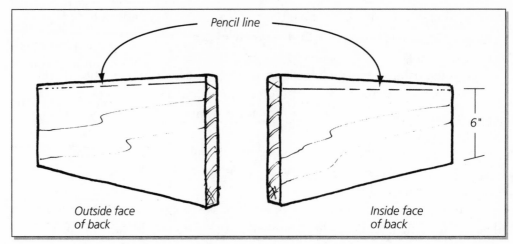

*Figure 30  Laying out
bevel on back*

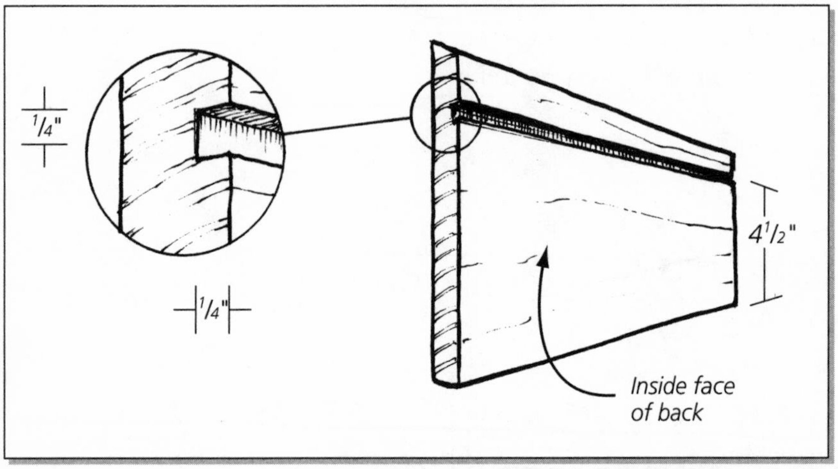

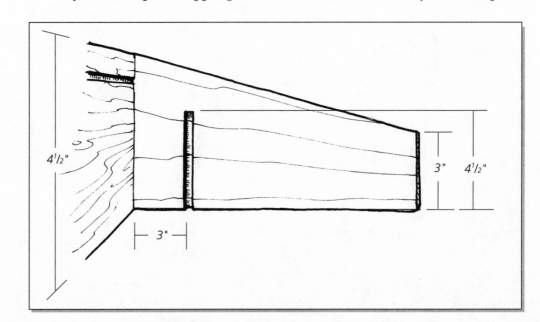

*Figure 31  Groove in
back*

*Figure 32  Location
of groove in side*

Cut rabbets in the front and back ends of the side pieces to receive the front and back pieces, and assemble all four pieces without glue. Using an adjustable bevel, transfer the angle of the sides to the top edges of the front and back (*Figure 30*). Mark this angle at *both* ends of the front and back pieces and connect the marks with a pencil line, thereby providing a line on both faces to plane to.

**Grooving**—A groove ¼ inch wide by ¼ inch deep must be made in the inside face of the back, 4½ inches up from the bottom (*Figure 31*). Use a marking gauge to mark this and then saw or chisel it out or—more easily—use a plough plane, but note that if a plough plane is used, this operation must be completed before the top edge is beveled in order that the fence have a square edge to run against.

Next, groove the two sides (*Figure 32*). Note that these grooves, also ¼ inch wide by ¼ inch deep, are stopped grooves and do not run all the way across the piece.

After the grooving is complete, glue and assemble with small finishing nails, preboring from front and back. If the rabbets have been cut well, the pieces will come together in a perfect rectangle, but be sure to check this with a trysquare used in each corner, or by measuring the diagonals, which should be equal.

The inside partition is most easily made from ¼-inch-thick stock, cut to the right height and length and then slipped into the grooves from beneath (*Figure 33*). Do not glue the partition for if it should shrink, it will split. Inserted dry, it is free to expand and contract at will.

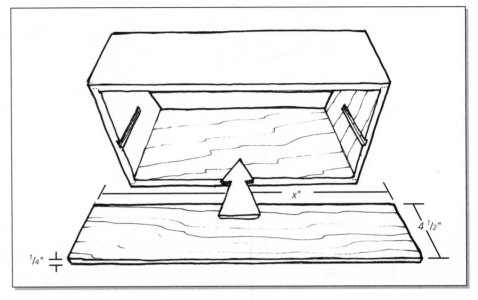

*Figure 33 Partition*

**The bottom**—Make the bottom ¼ inch larger all around than the area of the box. Around all four edges of the bottom, scribe a line ¼ inch up from its underside. Now center the box on the base and scribe a second line on the top surface of the bottom. This line is best made with a pencil. Use a block plane to smooth down to these lines, thus forming the bevel (*Figure 34*). By planing the long sides first, you will reduce the risk of splitting the endgrain of the short sides (ends).

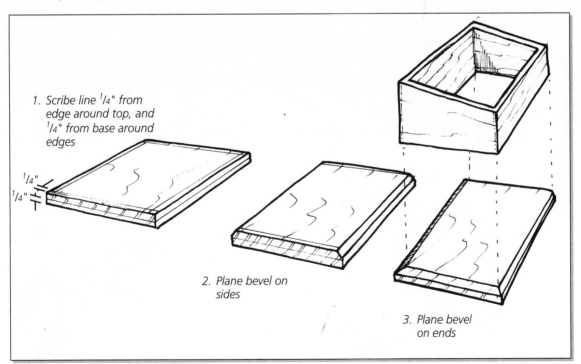

1. Scribe line ¹/₄" from edge around top, and ¹/₄" from base around edges

2. Plane bevel on sides

3. Plane bevel on ends

*Figure 34 Beveling base*

Fix the base to the sides by nailing up from underneath with 4d finishing nails as soon as everything has been planed and sanded smooth and clean.

**The inside compartment lid**—Cut the lid for the inside compartment to the dimensions shown at *Figure 35*, first by cutting to the correct length and width,

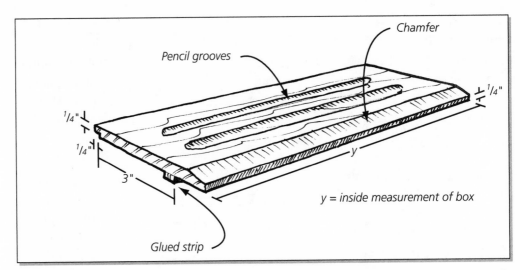

*Figure 35
Dimensions of
compartment lid*

and then by cutting the rabbet at the rear so that the lid fits easily into the ¼-inch groove in the back of the box. Bevel the front edge with the block plane, first marking the borders of the bevel with pencil lines. Glue the small stop-strip underneath, close enough to the front edge to prevent the lid from slipping out of its groove, but not so close that the lid cannot be removed and replaced easily. Finally, cut the pencil grooves, which should, of course, be wide enough to hold the average pen or pencil.

Use a gouge of an appropriate size to cut the grooves. Be sure to cut *with* the grain and stay within the guidelines you will have drawn with a pencil. Make a series of downward cuts along the entire length of the groove, and then remove the waste with the gouge held as flat as possible. Clean up the groove thus formed with a rubber, which is simply a piece of sandpaper folded over a piece of wood rounded to the required shape.

**The lid**—Making the lid is the last major operation. Cut the lid from the previously glued-up boards so that when laid on top of the box its front edge is flush with the front of the box, and the other three sides overlap ¼ inch.

Mark the central area, called the field or reserve, with a marking gauge set at 2 inches. Deepen the marks left by the pin of the marking gauge with a knife guided by a steel straightedge, followed by a chisel used on the waste side of the line, and a saw. Hold the saw perfectly level and cut no deeper than ⅛ inch (*Figure 36*).

Mark the outside edge of the lid in the same way as you marked the outside edge of the base, and then remove the waste with a block plane, working first with the grain, along the sides, and then cross-grain, across the ends (*Figure 37*). Use a bullnose rabbet plane to clean the area

*Figure 36 Laying out
panel field*

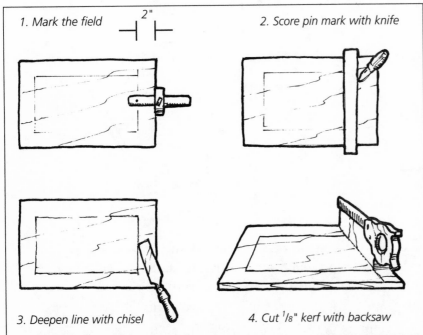

1. Mark the field 2"

2. Score pin mark with knife

3. Deepen line with chisel

4. Cut ⅛" kerf with backsaw

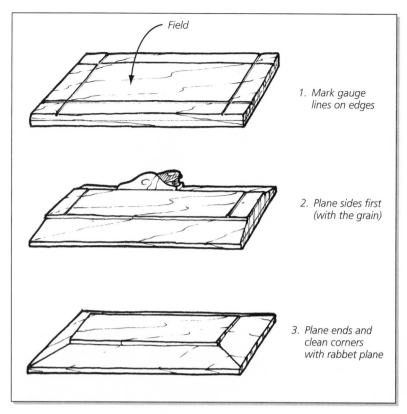

Field

1. Mark gauge lines on edges

2. Plane sides first (with the grain)

3. Plane ends and clean corners with rabbet plane

next to the scribed lines, because a regular block plane's iron will not reach into the corner.

When the raised panel has been cut and cleaned, place the lid on top of the box and use the adjustable bevel to mark the front edge of the lid at the point where it must be planed flush with the front of the box.

*Figure 37 Forming the field*

To fit the lid to the box, cut a 15-inch length of ½-inch piano-hinge and carefully mark around the hinge with a knife (*Figure 38*), centering its length along the front edge of the box so that the knuckle overlaps the front. Cut a rabbet for

the hinge to the depth of one leaf and screw the hinge to the box, using just a couple of screws in case any adjustment is necessary. Repeat the procedure on the lid, which will need to be supported while you do this. When you are sure that both parts of the hinge are properly positioned, insert the remainder of the screws.

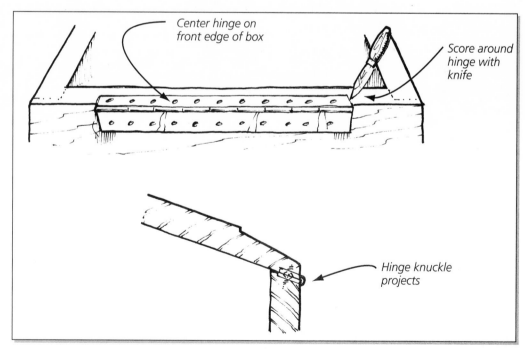

Center hinge on front edge of box

Score around hinge with knife

Hinge knuckle projects

*Figure 38 Positioning hinge*

Fill the nail holes with a colored wood filler that matches the walnut (or whatever species you may have used), and complete the box with the finish of your choice.

The floor of the box can be dressed up by covering a piece of cardboard cut slightly smaller than the inside dimensions of the box with felt or velvet.

## CUTTING LIST

1 lid ....................................13″ x 16½″ x ¾″

**Carcase:**

1 front ...............................16″ x 3″ x ¾″

1 back ...............................16″ x 6″ x ¾″

2 ends ...............................12″ x 6″ x 3″ x ¾″

1 base ...............................16½″ x 12½″ x ¾″

**Partition:**

1 partition upright ......................15″ x 4½″ x ¼″

1 compartment lid ......................14½″ x 3″ x ½″

1 compartment lid glued strip .............14½″ x ½″ x ¼″

**Hardware:**

1 piano-hinge ..........................14″ x ½″

# Legless coffee table

*Minimal production, maximum result*

Sometimes a design is the result not of realizing a preconceived picture of a particular piece, but of a pragmatic, trial-and-error approach worked out as you go along. Good design should always take construction into account, but construction alone should never be allowed to determine the design. The opposite is more usually the case: we stretch our construction abilities in order to realize a better design.

The legless coffee table was designed by starting with a need and attempting to satisfy this need with the minimum of effort. I needed to replace the coffee table that I had co-opted as a piano bench. It had to be fairly large and, most importantly, it had to appear almost immediately. There was no time for another lengthy project that would take weeks to germinate, months to execute, and further weeks to finish. I went to the shop and gazed unhappily at my small store of coffee-table–grade lumber. I was loath to waste such precious material on a quick knock-up—but how else to construct something that could be completed in a couple of days? Then I remembered the two planks of baywood a friend had brought me from Oregon.

**The path of least resistance**—Each plank was over 6 feet long and roughsawn to about 2½ inches thick. The planks were not straight-sided but interestingly curved, wider at one end than at the other. I had been thinking I would have to carry them over to a friend's shop, run them through his resaw bandsaw, cut them into straight boards, and then joint and surface them before I could use them for anything. The prospect of so much work had so far deterred me from using them. But one of them looked suspiciously like a possible coffee-table top. . . .

I laid the plank across the sawhorses and stared at it. It was almost the perfect width for a coffee table and its length closely matched the couch in front of which it was needed. Its gentle curves and gradually increasing width would also work well with the way the couch was arranged at right angles with a neighboring armchair. Best of all, its massive presence would complement the large stone fireplace that dominated the room it would occupy.

**The problem of support**—Pleased with what appeared to be an immediate solution to my need for an instant coffee table, I started to think about how the top might be supported. Cutting out legs from the second plank and joining them to a skirted frame was not too much work but would involve making sure that the top was perfectly flat so that it would fit securely. Since the top would be about 6 feet long and almost 2½ inches thick, the supporting frame would have to be similarly massive to restrain any possible warping and provide a solid base. Visions of Flintstone furniture that would require two elephants to move flashed before me and I rejected the standard construction. Perhaps I could saw the base plank into two slabs that would support the top transversely, one at each end. I played around with this idea for a while, making several drawings and even taking some chalk to the second plank to mark out where these slabs might come from. It wasn't a bad idea, but even if the supporting slabs were mortised into the underneath of the top, the extreme length and weight would still demand some extra form of connecting support, such as a connecting trestle-like member, either high up under the top or lower down, at the level of a foot rest, or perhaps two connecting members, one on each side of the slabs, let into the edge, and perhaps even supporting an additional shelf for magazine storage. But each solution involved more work. Every time I got close to structural sufficiency, I found I had created a project that would take just as long as a more conventional approach. And the point here was to create something quickly.

Finally I realized that the second plank, from which I had been thinking about sawing out various legs, slabs, and other forms of support, was massive enough to be stood on edge and support the first plank as is—almost. It was about the right height when stood on edge, and it was certainly thick enough to provide all the support necessary. Furthermore, using just one support like this would leave the top plank completely free to change dimension with no fear of anything being stressed or pulled apart. Additionally, the extra space for stretched-out feet that a legless construction would provide promised to be useful for a coffee table (*Figure 39*). The only remaining problem was how to get the supporting plank to stand securely on edge.

It was while thinking about how to trim the ends and sides of these two planks that the solution presented itself. Although I wanted to keep the overall curve of the top plank, I would still have to saw off a certain amount to produce the most felicitous shape, especially since I was now viewing the two planks as a whole and was trying to see how the one might best balance the other, both visually and structurally. Since my chief aim was to produce something with as little work as possible, I planned on removing the smallest amount I could get away with. This turned out to be a strip barely 3 feet long that tapered from about 3 inches thick to 1½ inches thick. I realized that by sawing this piece in half I could use one piece housed in the bottom of the supporting board to keep it upright and the other piece housed in the top edge to provide a pair of arms that would support the top (*Figure 40*). Both the top and the base would thus be supported at three points. Since one of the advantages of tripods over four-legged objects is that they will not rock no matter whether the surface they are resting

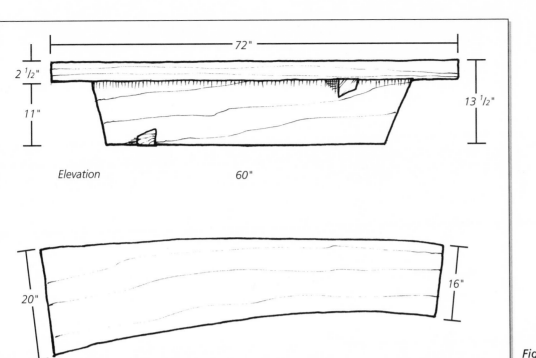

Elevation

Plan

*Figure 39  Coffee table dimensions*

on or their own individual lengths are uneven, this provided me with an excellent solution to the problem of leveling an object as massive as this coffee table.

**The top and base**—With a design that called for only four pieces and two joints, I felt I had successfully dealt with the structural part of the problem. All that remained was to use the chalk to mark exactly where I would trim the two planks. I wanted to keep the natural texture of the wood. After brushing the surfaces thoroughly before sawing to remove any edge-damaging grit or dirt, I was pleased to discover that the roughsawn surface was attractive enough to be left unplaned, thus further reducing the amount of work necessary. The planks had been sawed out of the tree with a chainsaw mill, and the irregular series of fan-shaped marks left were not too excessive and also presented an interesting texture. A few very light licks with my jack plane to remove the odd hair and whisker—not enough to produce any smoothly planed patches, but just to the point that you could run

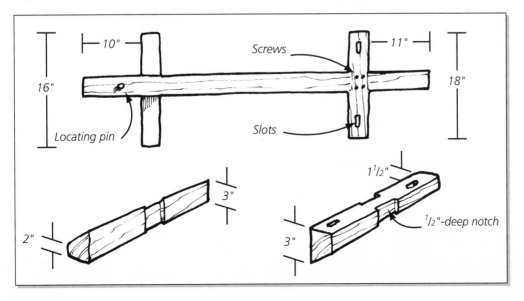

Screws

Locating pin

Slots

*Figure 40  Support dimensions*

your hand over the surface of the wood without fear of splinters—and the surface was ready for use. It was ideal in more ways than one: The mild but attractive grain was visible, the roughsawn texture was not only visually interesting but also provided a surface that would be difficult to damage the way a highly finished surface might be—ideal for putting your feet up—and slippery objects would be able to get a better grip.

To keep the edges consistent with the surface texture, I left these also as they came from the saw. The edges on the top plank turned out to be all fairly square, but the ends of the plank that became the base had been sawed somewhat out-of-square, both to the surfaces and the sides. I thought about this and decided the only edges that were critical were those that would bear against the floor and the top. The oddly angled ends and edges of the ends actually added interest, especially if I positioned the base so that the shorter side was down. Since the top was 1 foot longer overall than the base, this also added to the balance of the design as a whole and gave the table a profile somewhat reminiscent of an aircraft carrier.

The only finishing that was necessary was a ¼-inch chamfer around all exposed surfaces. This was planed by hand with a small block plane that could follow the curved edges. The chamfer had the effect of making the roughsawn material look nicely finished and suggested that the shapes had been purposely designed that way.

**The arms**—I sawed the strip I had removed from the base into two lengths. The first was 18 inches long: the width of the top at its narrow end. The second, cut from the thicker end of the taper, was only 16 inches long. The shorter but somewhat sturdier piece I let into the bottom edge of the base, 2 feet in from the sloping end. The longer piece, which contained most of the taper, running from 3 inches thick to a bare 1½ inches, I let into the top edge of the base 11 inches in from the opposite end.

The original strip had one edge out-of-square, and this angled edge was placed downwards in the case of the top arm and upwards in the case of the bottom arm, or foot. The arms were positioned so that the narrow edges of both pieces faced the respective ends of the base, giving the feeling of forwards movement to the shiplike quality of the table.

Like the base and top, the edges of the arms were given a ¼-inch chamfer, and their ends were smoothed with the block plane. These ends were thus the only perfectly smooth surfaces, but their relative smallness together with their inconspicuous placing lent an appropriate finishing detail, further emphasizing the appearance of a "finished" piece even though the shape was basically "natural."

The actual joint used here is a form of double housing-joint. Most of the joint is formed by notching out the respective edges of the base board, since the notch required does almost nothing to its integral strength. But a much smaller, ½-inch notch was made in the mating surface of the arms. This served the purpose of keeping the arm securely aligned by providing two extra bearing alignment surfaces. Marking the depth of the required notches needed to be done carefully, since the arms were neither square nor even in profile. But by making the small notch in the center of the arms first, a fixed reference was established from which the various depths of the notches required in the base could be measured. The entire process required the use of only four tools: a rule, a trysquare, a backsaw, and a 2-inch firmer chisel to pare away the waste between the two sawn lines.

The arms were set in place just a trifle proud of the top and bottom edges of the base to allow for any adjustment and to guarantee the tripod effect. The bottom edge rose slightly from the end opposite that into which the bottom arm had been housed. The top edge of the base was also slightly convex and required a little judicious planing at each end and at one side of the supporting arm before the top piece, supported by the ends of the arms and the opposite end of the top of the base, would rest securely.

**Final fixing**—Although the assembled table was indeed massive enough to be adequately stable, I wanted to avoid any disasters that might occur should anyone stand on the top. Consequently, I secured both the top and bottom arms with four 3-inch number 12 woodscrews each, angled into the corners of the joint. The top itself was kept in place by a 1-inch-diameter locating dowel that projected from the top of the base at the opposite end from the top arm, and fitted into a 1-inch-deep matching hole in the underside of the top. Two 3-inch-long, slot-screwed, roundhead woodscrews driven up through the bottom of each end of the top arm about 2 inches in from the ends completed the fixing and transformed the four parts into a single whole that when assembled did, indeed, need two people to move it.

A final check with block plane and a lightly waxed cloth to make sure all surfaces were clean and safe and pleasant to the touch and the project was complete. The entire process had taken less than three hours and the need had been filled with a design that while functional and stable had not been held hostage to complicated construction techniques.

## CUTTING LIST

| | |
|---|---|
| 1 top | . . . . . . . . . . . . . . . . . . . . . . . . . . . . . . .72″ x 20″ x 16″ x 2½″ |
| 1 base | . . . . . . . . . . . . . . . . . . . . . . . . . . . . .66″ x 60″ x 11″ x 2½″ |
| 1 top support | . . . . . . . . . . . . . . . . . . . . . .18″ x 3″ x 2½″ x 1½″ |
| 1 base support | . . . . . . . . . . . . . . . . . . . . . . . .16″ x 3″ x 2½″ x 2″ |
| 1 locating pin | . . . . . . . . . . . . . . . . . . . . . . . . .2- x 1-inch diameter |

# Side table

*The traditional approach*

In chapter 3 we looked at the way in which traditional design may be studied the better to understand construction methods that have stood the test of time. By incorporating such tried-and-true construction methods into the overall matrix of the design you stand a better chance of creating a successful piece of furniture. This chapter takes this concept a step farther. The side table provides an example of discovering how tradition and function can be found to go hand in hand.

By now it should be clear that not only well-made joinery but also joinery that is appropriate to the purpose the designed piece is expected to fulfill are necessary if the piece is to "work." We have all heard the saying "there is nothing new under the sun," but, the human spirit being what it is, there are always those reluctant to accept such a boring state of affairs. People are forever discovering new ways to solve old problems: New materials are made available, new tools invented, and new methods of work developed. Useful and exciting though this may be, it can be carried to extremes if it results in completely turning one's back on the past when faced with producing something—such as a design for a piece of furniture—that has been successfully done many times over. Without meaning to dampen anyone's creative enthusiasm for exploring new possibilities, it should be noted that attempting to solve an old, already successfully solved problem is hard to do. So often the attempt results merely in a different but less successful solution.

Nowhere is this more apparent than with traditional designs for basic furniture types. There are very good reasons for the ways in which certain traditional pieces are made—ways whose worth has been tested and proved often over centuries of careful refinement. Attempting to replicate the piece with anything other than a good understanding of the reasoning behind the traditional construction is a risky proposition. I am not merely talking about replicating extreme versions of a particular style such as might include ornately carved cabriole legs, intricately inlaid marquetry work, or finely turned sections, but about producing a piece to fulfill a basic, time-tested function. Such a piece is a simple table.

The demands of a table have not changed much since someone first had the idea of providing a stable, flat surface. Numerous ways have been worked out to produce this result, few more simple and more elegant than those practiced by the Shakers. The Shakers were morally opposed to gratuitous ornamentation, and in a period when other manufacturers were knee-deep in the excesses of Victorian ornament and stylistic gourmandizing their work stood out as one of the purest solutions to the utilitarian need for furniture. This side table is made in the Shaker style, and as such is best made from clear pine.

Once you understand the construction principles, the measurements given may be altered to suit your own needs and the availability of material, but as a starting point, let us assume the table will stand about 18 inches high and its top to be about 2 feet by 1½ feet. This is a good size for a bedside table, an end table, or even a small coffee table.

**Legs**—Make the legs from 2-inch by 2-inch clear pine, cutting all four legs from a single trued and squared length in order to ensure that they are all the same size. Mark the top ends. It is not important what the exact finished size is so long as all legs are equal. If the grain is at all pronounced, it will look best if all four legs are oriented in the same way relative to each other.

**Skirts**—The skirts, sometimes called aprons, that connect the legs are cut to length next. For dowel-jointing these to the legs it is best to use ¾ stock: wood that is nominally five-quarters of an inch thick. As when making the legs, it is easier to prepare the skirt as a single piece and before sawing the stock into individual skirt pieces, cut the groove described below under **Buttons.** Use your own judgment to determine the exact length and width of these pieces, but be sure to mark the pieces as shown in *Figure 41*.

Marking the various pieces is an important habit to develop if you want to avoid the disappointment of joining the wrong parts, especially after having lavished much attention on them. It is often difficult to remember in the middle of a project which face or edge of a particular piece you had originally decided would look best exposed, and annoying to discover that it has become oriented the wrong way in the finished piece. But don't get carried away; try to make marks on surfaces that will be hidden; if this is impracticable, make them lightly. All the marks so far needed on the legs and skirts should have been made on surfaces that will be hidden. A certain reverse snobbism exists with regard to marks such as the lines made for dovetail layouts found on some old pieces; if you feel such marks enhance the beauty or authenticity of a handmade piece, then use them, but remember that the goal is not really to

*Figure 41
Identifying relative
positions of legs and
aprons*

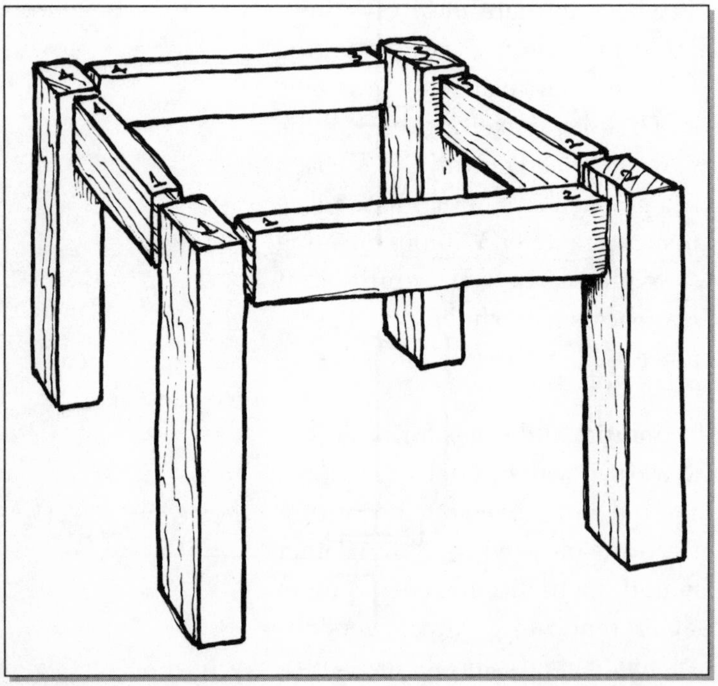

impress someone with
the difficulties of mak-
ing a piece so much as it
is to produce something
beautiful.

The skirts and legs
are joined by simple
dowel joints. As always,
make sure that the sur-
faces to be joined are perfectly square, trimming
the ends of the skirts if
necessary. Trim the short
skirts and the long skirts
in pairs to keep each
piece the same length.

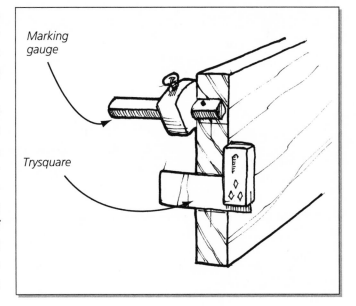

*Figure 42  Locating
dowel holes in apron*

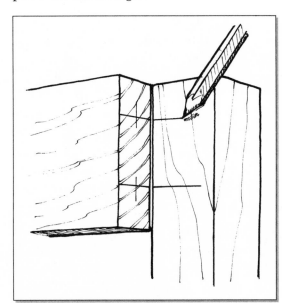

The top edge of the skirts must
be flush with the top of the legs,
which may be trimmed using a
shooting board. But it is a matter of
personal preference whether the
front of the skirt is flush with the
front of the leg, whether it is centered against the leg, or whether it is
positioned with a certain setback.
By positioning the skirts so their
*back* face is flush with the back of
the leg, an attractive setback at the
front will be formed. It also will

*Figure 43  Locating
dowel holes in leg*

*Figure 44  Dowel
offsets*

make marking the dowel holes easier since the
gauge, if used from the back of both members,
can be left at the same setting.

Use a trysquare and marking gauge as
shown in *Figure 42* to position the holes in the
center of the skirt's thickness, and then use
these marks to locate the dowel holes in the
legs (*Figure 43*). Note that although all dowel
holes should be located in the center of the
skirts' thickness, there should be a vertical offset between the position of the holes in adjacent skirts (*Figure 44*). To guarantee this
staggered effect, mark the position of the
needed holes in both ends of the long skirts
and the adjacent leg surfaces first, then locate
the holes in the short skirts.

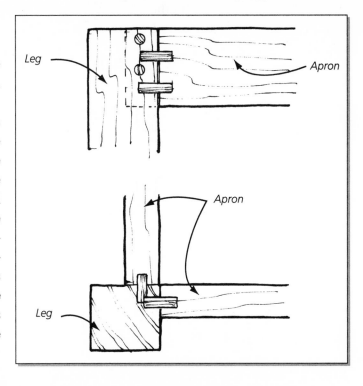

A doweling jig provides one of the surest ways to bore exact holes. If you lack one and must work freehand, however, be very careful to bore vertical holes to the appropriate depth, wrapping a piece of tape around the bit to act as a depth gauge. Prepare dowels slightly shorter than the combined depth in matching skirt and leg holes, and round their ends slightly. Lightly countersink the bored holes and glue grooved dowels into the skirt ends. The groove allows excess glue to escape from the bottom of the hole rather than possibly splitting the wood under pressure. Now assemble the legs to the long skirts, clamp, and allow to dry.

Next, join the two short skirts to one of the long assemblies, fit the remaining long assembly over the two ends, and clamp until dry.

If the table you are building is not too large, and if the skirts are stout enough, and if the ends have been prepared neatly, the assembly should be square with itself. Check this by measuring diagonally across the corners. If truly square, the measurements will be equal. Take care that excessive clamping pressure does not distort the assembly.

*Figure 45 Corner reinforcements*

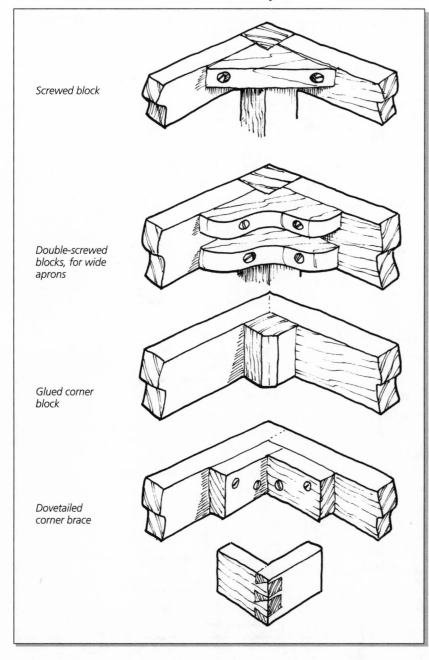

Screwed block

Double-screwed blocks, for wide aprons

Glued corner block

Dovetailed corner brace

**Corner blocks**—Although a small table joined this way should be strong enough for normal use, a larger table might require the use of corner blocks. Several varieties are illustrated in *Figure 45*, from a simple glued block to a stronger, dovetailed version screwed to the inside of the skirts. The glued block is common in old furniture, but be aware that, having been typically applied with its grain running perpendicular to that of the skirts, it is inherently likely to split. It was used this way because the long grain provides a more secure gluing surface and it is doubtless the quickest method. At the same time, any construction that requires a stronger corner block should probably have been mortise-and-tenoned rather than doweled in the first place.

**The table top**—If the table is small enough, it is possible that the top can be made from a single piece. But if, as is likely, two or more pieces are necessary to make up the required width, choose these pieces carefully.

Consider first that ¾ stock will look better with 2-inch-square legs than will ¾ stock. Since wood shrinks more across the grain than along the grain, orient the boards to run the length of the table rather than across it. Whether joining the boards with a simple butt-joint or with doweled edge-joints, allow for a substantial overhang on all four sides.

When the boards have been glued together and are out of clamps, trim the ends and then the sides. Next, plane the top smooth. While it is important to arrange the boards that form the top so that the grain at the ends is alternating (in order to equalize any cupping), and while you should have arranged the top grain to form the most pleasing pattern, you will now discover the advantage of having also arranged the boards so that their grain runs in a similar direction, making planing from one end more convenient (*Figure 46*). Meeting all these conditions at once is often not possible, however, and if because of alternating grain direction it proves difficult to plane the top without tear-out, you must either use a better-tuned plane (with a smaller mouth, a more closely set capiron, and an extremely sharp blade) or employ a scraper. While a scraper is more effective on close-grained hardwoods, you can also achieve good results with the careful use of a well-sharpened scraper on troublesome pine.

**Buttons**—Although the top must be secured firmly to the base, allowance must also be made for the top to expand and contract somewhat across the grain or it will surely split. A simple way to do this is with buttons, screwed to the underside of the top, that engage a groove cut in the inside of the skirts. The buttons keep the top firmly in place, and they can also slide in the grooves as the top

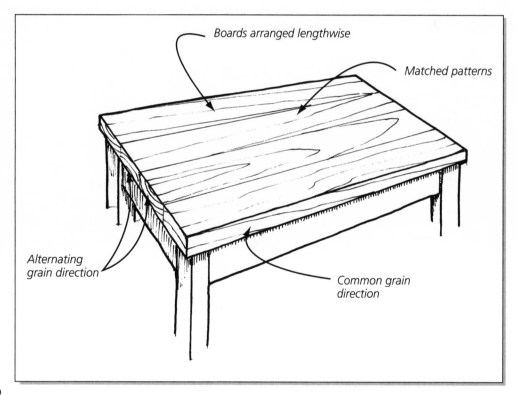

changes dimension with no damage to either top or base.

The groove in which the buttons slide should be sufficiently far from the top inside edge of the skirt to allow the buttons, when inserted in the groove, to pull the top down tightly to the top edge of the skirt as they are screwed to the underside of the top. Unless you anticipate any upwards warping of the long sides of the top, it is not really necessary to secure the top to the long skirts, but if you do, be sure to position the buttons with some space between the ends of their tongues and the bottom of the groove to allow for expansion of the top. Similarly, make sure that the grooves are deep enough to prevent the buttons from slipping out if the top contracts.

*Figure 46 Optimum grain arrangement*

The buttons are best made from scrap pieces of hardwood, cut so that the grain runs into the tongue and not across it. Forming the tongue on a long strip of scrap and then sawing off individual buttons (*Figure 47*) is the quickest way to produce as many as you need. They do not need to be longer than a couple of inches, so be sure to prebore the screw holes, and use screws shorter than the combined thickness of button and top. The number of buttons required is dictated by the size of the table; a top 18 inches wide should need no more than three at each end.

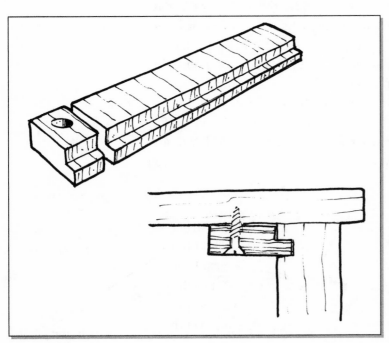

*Figure 47 Button construction*

**Finishing**—Soften all edges and corners by wiping them with fine sandpaper. To prevent the bottoms of the legs from chipping with rough usage, chamfer the bottom square lightly and consider fitting small furniture glides to enable the table to be moved smoothly and silently. There are several varieties available; besides protecting the bottoms of the legs, they also protect the floor from being scraped and facilitate moving the piece should it be heavy.

It is best not to leave pine unfinished unless you intend to scrub it clean periodically or it will quickly become dirty and stained. You may apply various finishes, including varnish, shellac, or polyurethane, but for a beautiful Shaker-style finish, which will gradually turn the pine to a mellow pale orange color, rub in some boiled linseed oil, a little at a time, on all surfaces.

There are two kinds of linseed oil generally available: raw and boiled. The boiled, being somewhat thinner in consistency, is more penetrating and quicker-drying. In the long run, however, it is just as effective to use raw linseed oil, perhaps thinning the first coat with a little turpentine. The process can be repeated from time to time over the years and whenever repair is necessary, but beware of applying too much too often. It will build up and produce a sticky, dirt-attracting skin that you will have to scrape clean. The secret is in constant, patient rubbing.

## CUTTING LIST

1 top . . . . . . . . . . . . . . . . . . . . . . . . . . . . . . . .18″ x 24″ x 1¹⁄₁₆″
4 legs . . . . . . . . . . . . . . . . . . . . . . . . . . . . . . . .18″ x 2″ x 2″
2 short skirts . . . . . . . . . . . . . . . . . . . . . . . . . .14″ x 4″ x 1¹⁄₁₆″
2 long skirts . . . . . . . . . . . . . . . . . . . . . . . . . .20″ x 4″ x 1¹⁄₁₆″
16 pins . . . . . . . . . . . . . . . . . . . . . . . . . . . . . .1″ x ½″ diameter
6 buttons . . . . . . . . . . . . . . . . . . . . . . . . . . . . .1¼″ x ¾″ x ¾″

**Hardware:**
4 furniture glides

# Parson's table

*The essence of simplicity*

In contrast to the traditional approach taken in the design and construction of the side table discussed in chapter 6, the parson's table described in this chapter focuses attention on another aspect of design. A parson's table is the name given to a simple table, usually square, supported by a leg at each corner. It is hard to think of anything more straightforward when considering the possibilities for a table—a flat surface supported at a given height—and yet there is more to such apparent simplicity than meets the eye.

Very often we make things for structural or aesthetic reasons and design our work accordingly. The acquisition of a new tool or the learning of a new technique inspires us to design and build something to try out the tool or practice our skill. As wood-lovers, we are often lured by our appreciation of the material into creating something simply to celebrate the exquisite grain or other properties of a choice piece of wood. What we build may be functional, and we may even have a need for the finished object, but that this is not the prime motivation is demonstrated by the fact that need alone would hardly have dictated countless hours spent constructing something that might have been obtained ready-made far more cheaply. This is probably why we are woodworkers in the first place; we like the materials and processes. The ability to produce something useful is only a secondary benefit.

But occasionally a project comes along in which function *is* the motivating force and chief consideration. Caring about our material and the way we build things will still influence what we make, but technical excess for the sheer joy of woodworking and clever design simply to display the beauty of the wood are no longer the name of the game. Such was the genesis of this coffee table. What was required was the simplest, most straightforward design consistent with structural integrity and the character of the material that was available to make it.

Almost by definition, therefore, a parson's table was the chief candidate for this design (*Figure 48*), but seeking to keep the design and the construction as

*Figure 48
Dimensions*

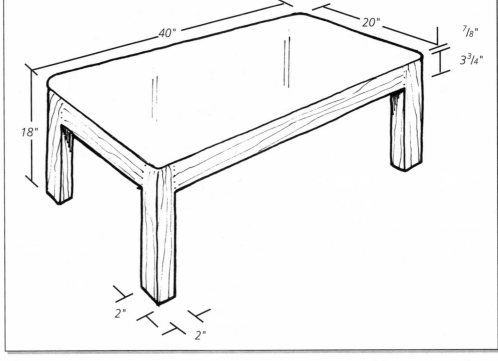

simple as possible, and recognizing the greater importance of function over form, can be far from easy. Simplicity is often quite complicated!

**The elements of simplicity**—Simplicity as defined above includes several elements that sometimes tend to be at odds with one another: a straightforward design that serves the required function as well as possible; a structure that supports this and which at the same time is as easy to build as possible and also possessed of sufficient integrity not to fall apart at the first use; and the use of a given material—in this case, oak—that is consistent with the two previous requirements as well as being used to its own best advantage.

**Design**—The design of this table would at first glance seem to be a perfect opportunity for applying the well-known maxim "form follows function." The function of a coffee table represents no great mystery; all that is required is a fairly low, stable, flat surface that can be conveniently positioned in front of a couch or by an armchair. So long as flatness and height are provided, the actual shape of this surface is susceptible to a wide variety of interpretations. But since we are also looking for the simplest structure, wild or subtle outlines and complicated or ingenious supports must be avoided. We need a simple flat surface, simply supported, and simply made.

Basic geometric shapes suggest themselves: circles, squares, ovals, and triangles. Theologians have argued—and their arguments have been the basis for much architectural design, especially during the great period of cathedral building—that nothing is simpler than the circle. It was supposed to represent divinity, infinity, and perfection. But its perfection is often a great mystery, as is the construction of ovals, whose parameters are endless. It is considerably easier for most woodworkers to construct rectilinear forms since triangles are not the easiest form to position in front of a couch, we are left with squares and rectangles. The advantage of a rectangular coffee table in front of a rectangular couch is obvious.

Having decided on a rectangular surface, we are now faced with the problem of how to support this as simply as possible. One solution would be to make the surface thick enough so that its top was at the right height. Nothing could be simpler than this, and both stability and ease of construction would be attained. But this would be impracticable for other reasons: It would require excessive material and no one would be able to put their feet under the table.

The next simplest solution would be to provide a single, central support, but this might introduce problems of stability and consequent construction complications. As we investigate the possibilities of other leg arrangements, it soon becomes apparent that a leg at each corner is the easiest way out. And so we arrive at an elongated parson's table.

**Structure**—The next problem is to determine the simplest way to connect the four legs to the rectangular surface—without resorting to nails or other crude approaches—that will provide stability and structural integrity.

There are many ways to join an upright securely to a flat surface, and choosing any one of these in combination with four legs of exactly the same length might provide the desired stability for a while, but structural integrity is a different matter. We need to be concerned not only with the engineering of the desired structure, but also the nature of the material. Wood may contract and expand in response to changing ambient moisture content over a very long time—centuries, in fact, as disastrous checking in ancient pieces suddenly brought into different surroundings can prove. Moreover, wood moves differently with and along the grain (*Figure 49*). If several pieces were all attached to one another with their grain running in the same direction, any movement would result in all pieces moving in the same way. Provided the movement was unrestrained, little damage would result. But when pieces of wood are firmly connected so that their respective grain directions are at right angles to each other,

*Figure 49 Wood movement*

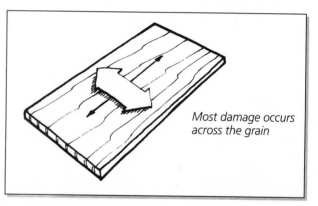

*Most damage occurs across the grain*

*Figure 50 Methods of dealing with wood movement*

trouble can be expected, as the different movements inexorably result in splitting or separation.

Accommodating wood movement is at the heart of all woodworking technique. Joinery and cabinetmaking were both developed to produce joints and wooden constructions that, although sturdy and stable, could accommodate the dimensional changes in the various members of any given piece of furniture (*Figure 50*). This then becomes the central structural problem of

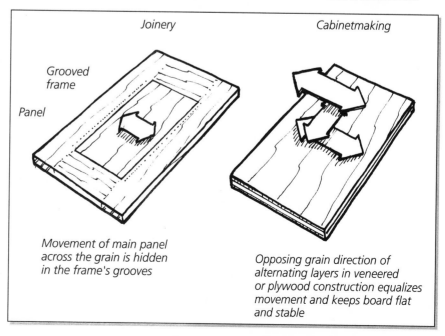

*Joinery*

*Cabinetmaking*

*Grooved frame*

*Panel*

*Movement of main panel across the grain is hidden in the frame's grooves*

*Opposing grain direction of alternating layers in veneered or plywood construction equalizes movement and keeps board flat and stable*

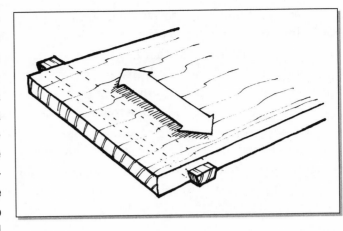

*Figure 51  Sliding-
dovetail cleat*

our design, which consists of various members oriented at right angles to each other.

If we can attach a single-piece top in such a way that it is free to contract and expand while remaining firmly connected to the legs, we will have done much to ensure the structural integrity of our design without having to resort to more complicated techniques such as varieties of frame-and-paneling and veneering. These are considerably more time-consuming than is preparing a single-piece top.

The Shakers, who were masters of simplicity, were fond of sliding-dovetail cleats that kept a board-top flat and attached to a base without restricting its movements (*Fig-*

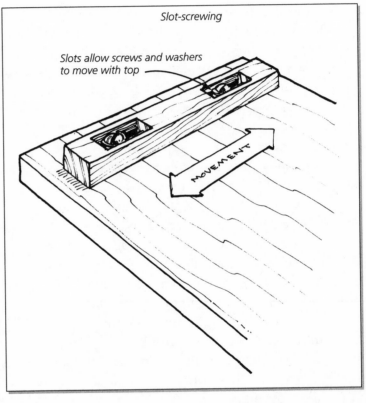

Slot-screwing

Slots allow screws and washers
to move with top

MOVEMENT

*Figure 52
Slot-screwing*

*ure 51*). But this requires a certain amount of time to make with care. Slot-screwing is another technique whereby a flat surface may be held to a base and still be free to move (*Figure 52*), but this too requires several operations to accomplish. A simpler method is to connect the legs with a narrow skirt, grooved at its top inside edge, and attach the top to the skirt, with wooden buttons or with metal hardware that slides in the grooves (*Figure 53*).

**The material**—Lastly, we have to consider the material itself. Different species of wood have different characteristics, are better suited for some purposes than for others, and behave differently under similar conditions. Using softwood for a project subjected to heavy wear would be a bad idea. Highly figured and strongly colored wood in a subdued setting might represent an unpleasant contrast. Making a relatively unimportant piece out of an extremely expensive and rare piece of wood would also be inappropriate. In this instance, oak was chosen because it was available, it was certainly strong enough to be used for a coffee table, and it matched the rest of the furniture in the intended location.

At the same time it has to be remembered that oak is open-grained and has a pronounced figure. Both these points can affect a design if they are not worked with sympathetically. For example, designing something in oak with many parts requires that careful attention be paid to the grain pattern or it might overpower the structural design. While oak is good to carve because its hardness makes clean cuts easier, its open grain is not well suited to very fine detail. Once again, simplicity becomes a virtue.

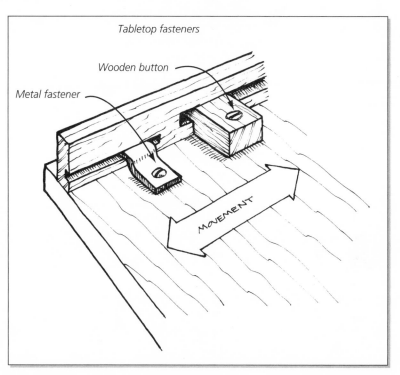

Figure 53 Buttons and tabletop fasteners

**Construction**—With all the foregoing in mind, the coffee table was designed as illustrated and constructed as follows: The length and width of the rectangular shape having been decided upon, and enough material chosen and put aside for this purpose, attention was first given to the base, as it is easier to adjust the finished size of the top to the base than vice-versa.

**The legs**—The legs were made from a single length of ¾ oak. Because this particular piece of 2-inch-thick oak was a little over 4 inches wide, it needed only to be as long as the combined length of two legs, since it could then be resawed to make four.

It was first planed flat and straight on one face. A jointer might have been used for this, or even the tablesaw, but 3 feet is not too much to plane, and a nice surface is left from the plane iron. Next, one adjacent side was planed not only flat and true but also perfectly perpendicular to the finished face, checking frequently with a trysquare. The remaining face was now planed to be perpendicular to the first side.

Using a marking gauge set at a little over 2 inches, lines were scribed down both faces and connected around one end to serve as a guide for resawing by hand, although once again there were other options available, including the table saw and the bandsaw. After resetting the marking gauge to exactly 2 inches, all four sides of both pieces were scribed, and then planed where necessary to these lines.

Now the two pieces were sawed in half to produce four, care being taken that each end was first marked perfectly square with a trysquare.

Finally, before laying out the legs for joining to the skirt, they were looked at from all sides to determine which way round and which way up the grain would look best. This is a subjective procedure and ultimately depends on what looks best to you; different arrangements are likely to be preferred by different people. It is extremely unlikely, however, that if the process is omitted an arrangement will result that is acceptable; leave the orientation of such strongly figured wood to chance and one or more pieces will surely stand out oddly.

The legs had been sawed from a piece of riftsawn stock. This is a method of sawing in which the growth rings of the tree are diagonal to the section (*Figure 54*). Consequently, all four legs still had diagonal endgrain, and no one side dis-

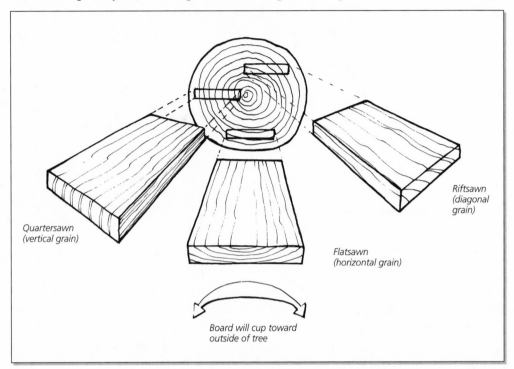

Quartersawn
(vertical grain)

Riftsawn
(diagonal
grain)

Flatsawn
(horizontal grain)

Board will cup toward
outside of tree

*Figure 54
Relationship of grain
to board conversion*

played the characteristic medullary rays of quartersawn oak. There were, nevertheless, sides marked more strongly than others, and these were oriented toward the inside in an effort to present the most regular faces to the more visible out-

side. The legs thus arranged were grouped together and their top ends marked (*Figure 55*) so that this order would be clear throughout subsequent construction.

**The skirts**—The narrow skirts that connect the legs, and to which the top is connected, were prepared in a similar manner to the legs. Starting with a piece twice as wide as the required finished width and as long as the combined length of one front skirt and one side skirt, the outside face side was planed first, then one edge, exactly square to the face, was finished, and then the inside face. Finally, the two pieces were ripped down their centers. The four resultant pieces were considered for the best grain orientation, designated appro-

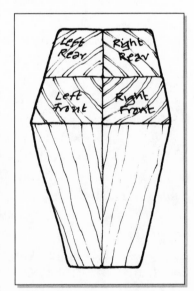

*Figure 55 Leg
arrangement*

priately, and then marked to the finished width and planed carefully to this line.

The width had been determined carefully to balance the thickness of the legs, taking into account the expected finished thickness of the top. Anything less and the skirts would have had an appearance too insubstantial; anything more and they would have looked too heavy. That what looked just right also left enough width for the biscuit joinery planned to connect them to the legs, and for

THE
THINKING
MAN'S
CHEST

TABLETOP
SIX-BOARD
CHEST

LARGE
SIX-BOARD
CHEST

DESK BOX
(CLOSED)

DESK BOX
(OPEN)

LEGLESS
COFFEE
TABLE

## SHAKER-STYLE
## SIDE TABLE

## PARSON'S
## TABLE

*Woody Packard
photograph*

PEPSYIAN

BOOKCASE

*Andrew Wainwright*
*photograph*

TRAVELING
TRESTLE TABLE

*Woody Packard
photograph*

DINING TABLE

*Woody Packard
photograph*

GLAZED
CREDENZA

*Woody Packard
photograph*

STANDING
CABINET

*Woody Packard
photograph*

# STEREO UNIT

*Andrew Wainwright*
*photograph*

GOTHIC
ARMCHAIR
FRAMEWORK

GOTHIC
ARMCHAIR

*Woody Packard
photograph*

the groove to be made on their upper inside surfaces, was also confirmed. But what was immaterial was the exact thickness: So long as there was a minimum of ¾ inch to secure a single biscuit and to provide for a safe groove about ⅜ inch deep, each skirt might, in fact, be a different thickness. Additionally, the inside face need be only roughly finished since it would never be visible.

The groove for the table fasteners was made by setting the tablesaw fence ⅜ inch from the inside face of the saw blade, setting the depth of cut to ⅜ inch, and then running a couple of saw kerfs—adjusting the fence after the first cut—along the inside faces of the skirts near their top edges.

For successful biscuit-joinery, mating surfaces must be perfectly flat and square. To guarantee that the ends of the skirts met these criteria, each pair of skirts was trimmed together on a very carefully adjusted tablesaw. A slower method would have been to square off the ends with a trysquare and trim to this line with a block plane, always working in from the edges, and ideally using a shooting block if one was available.

If several attempts had been necessary to obtain perfectly square-ended pairs, consequently shortening the length each time, no great harm would have been done, as the top had not yet been made and could easily be adjusted to fit.

Number 2 biscuits were used with a plate-joiner to attach the skirts to the legs in pairs, each pair being glued, assembled, clamped, and left to dry before both pairs were assembled together.

This sounds straightforward, but implicit in successful assembly is perfect alignment. This may be achieved by assembling each pair, and finally both pairs together, on a known flat surface. Make sure that all four legs touch the ground and that the rectangle formed by the skirt-connected legs is indeed a rectangle and that diagonal measurements taken from opposite corners match exactly, adjusting the positions of the clamps if necessary to achieve this.

**The top**—No matter how many pieces may be necessary to make the top large enough to cover the base exactly, they must all be arranged as felicitously as possible. Once again, this is a question of personal choice, but almost any thought given to this matter will produce a happier result than if none is given.

There are various opinions about how the grain should be oriented in adjacent pieces forming a flat surface. This stems from the fact that an unrestrained flatsawn section will tend to cup towards the side that, when it was still part of the tree, faced the outside (*Figure 55*). Some people recommend joining pieces all the same way so that any cupping will result in a single large cup, which can perhaps be easily controlled at its center or edges. Others recommend alternating pieces so that cupping is spread out among the components, creating a washboard effect, but an overall smaller deformation. You can avoid the problem entirely if you join wood so that its cross-section

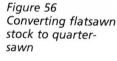

*Figure 56
Converting flatsawn
stock to quarter-
sawn*

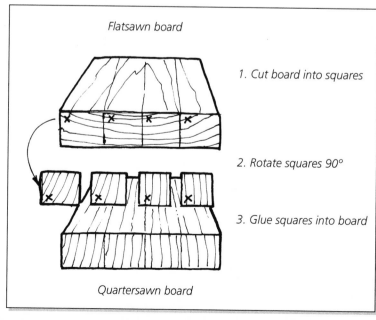

Flatsawn board

1. Cut board into squares

2. Rotate squares 90°

3. Glue squares into board

Quartersawn board

most closely resembles quartersawn lumber, even if this means sawing up the available stock and regluing it (*Figure 56*). By doing this you will, of course, end up with sidegrain forming the surface, a felicitous effect in this case where we are aiming for simplicity and regularity.

No matter how you glue up the top, cupping should not be too great a problem providing the top is surfaced flatly and then attached to the base properly. The finished thickness as given is also not critical providing it looks right.

Before rounding the edges, cut the top to size simply by scribing around the base placed upside down on the top, leaving an extra ⅛ inch all round.

**Edge treatment**—In order to keep the top as simple as possible and to allow for movement without periodic unsightly misalignments between the edges of the top and the base, the edges of the top were rounded to form an almost complete half-circle, and the top edge of the base was also rounded. Do this with appropriately sized round-over bits in a router; by chamfering the corners with a block plane and then completing the round by planing additional facets and sanding; or by running the various sections through a shaper. This effectively disguises the exact point at which the top meets the base, so that any changes in this relationship are hard to detect. In order to impart a feeling of integral consistency to the whole piece, the outside corners of the legs were rounded to the same degree as was the top of the base. All other edges were merely softened slightly.

**Assembly and finishing**—With a couple of clamps positioned judiciously to hold the top in position on the base, tabletop fasteners were attached to the underside of the top so that their offset ends engaged the slots in the skirts. Remember that the top is liable to change size most across the grain, and that fixing a screw at the center of each end will force this movement to take place equally on both sides.

Finishing consisted simply of multiple coats of Watco™, applied thinly and rubbed well at daily intervals. Four coats are sufficient for average protection; more coats afford more protection and also increase the shine.

## CUTTING LIST

| | |
|---|---|
| 1 top | .20″ x 40″ x ⅞″ |
| 4 legs | .18″ x 2″ x 2″ |
| 2 short skirts | .16″ x 3¼″ x ⅞″ |
| 2 long skirts | .36″ x 3¼″ x ⅞″ |
| 6 tabletop fasteners (or 6 buttons) | .1¼″ x ¾″ x ¾″ |

# Sound shelving

*Designing to a need*

The most satisfying projects are often the result of a serendipitous find and an urgent need. In this case it was the happy marriage of a couple of cherry boards I inherited by chance and the pressing need for a better way to house my growing collection of stereo components. The cat's habit of jumping on the unprotected record turntable was doing it no good, and the compact disc player stacked on top of the cassette player, in turn stacked on top of the amplifier and receiver, was also bad for the health of these expensive items. I didn't want to build an entire entertainment center, which might include the television and videocassette recorder and speakers, but I did need to get the audio components off the coffee table and shelve them somewhere convenient and protected.

**The material**—The cherry consisted of two irregular, 6-foot boards. Both boards were considerably narrower at one end than at the other and it occurred to me that by removing a tapered section from the narrow end of each board, reversing it, and joining it to the wider end, I could produce a pair of well-proportioned, sloping sides (*Figure 57*). The resulting shape had several advantages, of which the most appealing was the feeling and look of balance. The last thing wanted when designing shelving for electronic equipment is something that might tip over. These sides were sufficiently broader at the base than at the top to be almost as stable as the pyramids. The sloping front also made access to the different components equally easy, and the sloping back provided room for all the wires and connecting cables while still permitting the unit to be pushed, at its base, securely against the wall.

Since much of the shelving is necessarily covered by what sits on it, buying extra cherry seemed a little wasteful. Pine is cheaper and readily available at lumberyards. The color also provides a pleasant contrast to cherry. All that was needed was a single 14-foot piece of 1-by-12 (a nominal dimension that typically measures ¾ inch by 11½ inches). By careful cutting it was possible to avoid most of the small knots that are included in what is usually called number one grade. Those that were left were in places that weren't visible. Buying clear pine would have been considerably more expensive but is still usually cheaper than cherry, and in many parts of the country it can be hard to find cherry as wide as pine.

**The design**—Since audio components need to be connected together, the shelves were designed to be backless. A backless shelf unit, however, poses problems of side-to-side stability. One way to solve this is to add a diagonal brace. A better way is to provide at least a partial back. By designing the shelving to start at waist

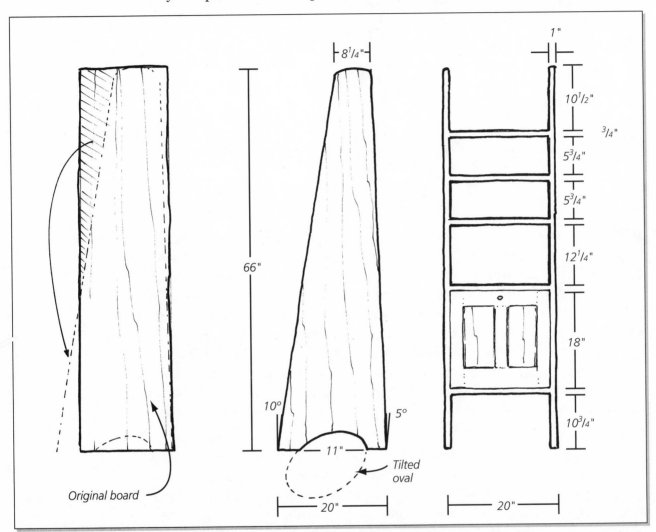

*Figure 57*
*Origination and dimensions of sound shelving unit*

level—thereby enabling each component to be reached without excessive bending—adequate space for a small cupboard was left beneath the lowest shelf. The back of this cupboard provides the needed sideways stability. The cupboard forms a useful storage area for various accessories such as record-cleaning equipment, headphones, and manuals.

One last consideration in this era of transience influenced the design: the need for easy transportation. Knock-down furniture is much easier to move or store than are solid pieces, that take up more space and remain vulnerable to damage while being manhandled in and out of apartments and moving vans. Joining the shelves to the sides with sliding dovetails accomplished this, and also made assembly easier. None of the shelves is permanently fixed in place. The dovetails are stopped 1 inch short of the front edge of the sides (*Figure 58*). This allows the shelves to be pushed firmly into position and guarantees that all are equally aligned. The paneled front is hinged to the bottom shelf and can be easily disassembled by unscrewing the hinges, or transported folded against it. The paneled back, which is the key to the entire unit's stability, is secured between the two bottom shelves by two screws through each shelf.

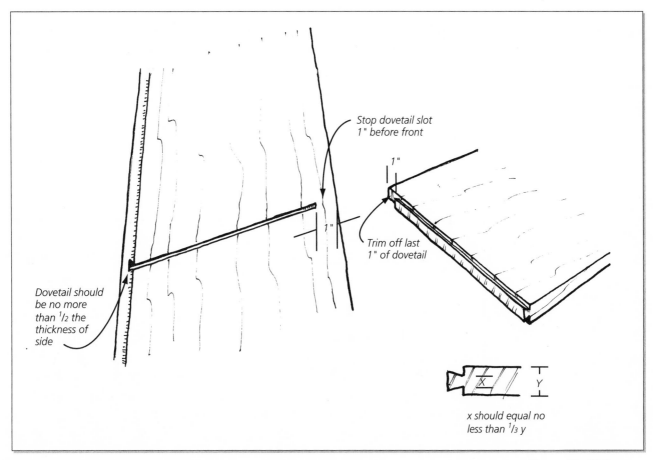

Stop dovetail slot
1" before front

1"

1"

Trim off last
1" of dovetail

Dovetail should
be no more
than ¹/₂ the
thickness of
side

x should equal no
less than ¹/₃ y

*Figure 58 Sliding
dovetail details*

**Dimensions and methods**—You may alter the measurements given here to suit your own preferences, bearing in mind that the size of audio components is relatively standard. Use these measurements as a starting point; aim for a pleasing shape while maintaining stability. The exact shape of the sides will depend on the material available.

The dimensions of the sides as shown were largely the result of the size of the original boards. One important fact that made the construction of sliding dovetails easy was the 1-inch thickness of the finished material, but with a little care the same dovetails can be cut using ¾-inch-thick material for shelves and sides.

It is much faster—and the results are more likely to be evenly accurate—if you cut the sliding dovetails with a router, or on a shaper, rather than by the traditional hand method. All other operations and procedures needed to build this unit are equally easily undertaken using hand tools or powertools, depending on what you are comfortable with and what you have at your disposal. Do not feel bound by any particular method.

**The sides**—Prepare the sides first. Cut and join where necessary and surface both sides to be as flat as possible. Cut out the slightly off-center half-oval in the bases, using a thin lath to lay out the curve on one side and then using this side to lay out the curve on the other side. The bottoms of the sides are left flat but the top, front, and back edges may be given a shaped profile. A 1-inch round plane was used on the piece shown, working to lines drawn ¼ inch in from the edge, a file being first used on the top before the plane was employed, to produce a gently rounded profile. Other methods include using a block plane to produce a chamfer, or a shaped bit in a router, or even leaving the edge flat.

The exact shape and angles at which the front and back slope are not critical, but it is important to make both sides identical. If you decide on dimensions other than those given, remember that most audio components are about 10 inches deep; leave at least this depth for the top shelf, or whatever stands on it will hang over the edge. Since turntables are the most variable in size, and in any event are at least large enough to accommodate a 12-inch record, it is best to design the lowest shelf to be deep enough to hold this component. Most components average 17 inches in width; when deciding how wide the shelves should be, include an extra inch on either side of your widest component. It is also important to leave 1 inch of air space above each component for ventilation. You will need more room above the turntable, if this is part of your system, to permit its lid to be raised or removed.

Having worked out the dimensions for all the above, design the bottom of the cupboard so that it looks good proportionately while being as big as possible for greatest stability, and finishes at a height above the floor that gives the unit the right overall appearance of balance. This is, of course, completely subjective. I like a little room beneath the cupboard to complement the space between the sides at the top of the unit, but you may even prefer to omit the cutout at the bottom of the sides and have the cupboard reach all the way to the floor.

Whatever dimensions you settle on, lay out the positions of the shelves on the insides of the sides as accurately as possible. Double-check by comparing both sides to each other. Use a sliding bevel set to the angle of the slope to determine true horizontality, but remember that you may have different angles at the front and back.

Mark a line parallel to the front edge of the sides across the shelf layout lines, 1 inch in from the front. The female section of all the dovetails will be stopped at this point, guaranteeing equal alignment of all shelves. Insert a ½-inch dovetail bit in the router and clamp a guide across the side so that the bit cuts exactly in the middle of each shelf. Make sure at least a third of the sides' thickness remains at the bottom of the dovetail slot.

A final sanding of the sides at this point is useful to remove any feathering that may have occurred along the dovetail slot, and then the sides can be considered finished.

**The shelves**—Prepare as many shelves as are necessary to the required width, joining pieces where needed to produce the right depth. Bevel their front and back edges to match the slope of the front and back of the sides. With the dovetail bit in the router at the same depth as was used to cut the female portion of the dovetail, cut the male portion of the joint in the ends of the shelves. This requires two passes, one on each side. Use two pieces of scrap clamped to either side of the ends to provide a stable bearing for the router's shoe (*Figure 59*). Make sure these pieces are perfectly level with the end and mark them so the same piece is always used on the same side.

Lay out the position of the male dovetail on the end of the shelf. After the two scrap pieces are clamped in place, adjust the router's fence to cut the bottom side first. Cut the bottom side on all shelf ends before cutting the top side, mak-

ing sure you keep the scrap pieces clamped to the same sides. This will guarantee that even if the first complete dovetail is less than perfect, all shelves will at least be at the same height. Making a trial joint on a piece of scrap the same thickness as the shelves will demonstrate whatever adjustment may be necessary to the router's fence when it comes to cutting the top half of the dovetail.

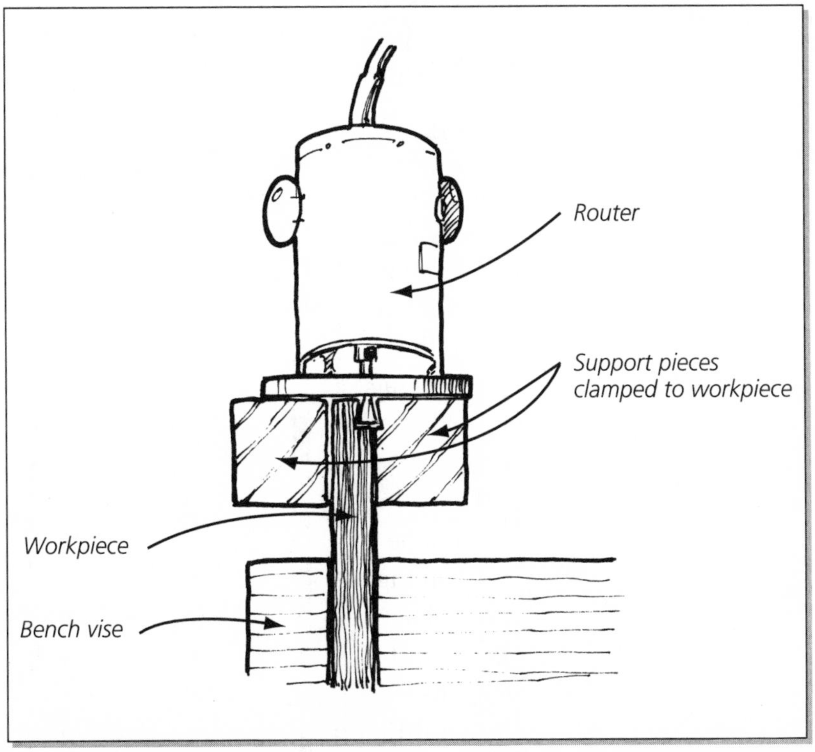

Finally, pare back the first 1 inch of the dovetail from the front edge of every shelf and test every shelf in its matching slot in both sides. Plane, scrape, or sand, according to your preference, every shelf to finished perfection, and assemble everything. Although the joints should be tight enough to require only light malleting home, using a piece of scrap to protect the beveled edges, the unit will doubtless wobble somewhat from side to side. The back will take care of this.

*Figure 59 Method of supporting router when cutting sliding dovetails*

**The cupboard back and door**—Measure the distance between the bottom two shelves and make a mortise-and-tenoned frame to fit (*Figure 60*). Allowing an extra ⅛ inch all around is a good idea, because the finished frame can then be trimmed to fit perfectly, especially by beveling the top and bottom edges. This is necessary since the back should slope at the same angle as the back of the sides (*Figure 61*). To avoid having to join material in order to make a single panel wide enough to fill the frame. and also because I felt it looked better I fitted a central muntin in the frame and made two smaller panels.

After the various framing members have been cut to length and width, plough a groove in all inside edges to accommodate the panel, or panels. The job is easiest if the groove is centered and also made the same width as the mortises. Working with handtools, this means using the same width plough iron as mortise chisel, keeping the mortise gauge set to the same width when marking mortises, tenons, and the panel groove, and being sure to use the mortise gauge always from the same face. If you are using ¾-inch-thick material, ¼-inch, centered tenons work well.

Center the ¼-inch tongue formed around the edge of the panel and allow a little space for the panel to expand should its moisture content increase, but not so much that, should the reverse happen and the panel shrink across its width, it will pop out of the frame. Since a certain amount of movement is inevitable, forming a bead and quirk down both long-grain sides on the face side of the panel will mask any variation in width. A ¼-inch wooden beading plane is an extremely easy tool to use, and not too hard to find at fleamarkets or in antique stores. The same effect can also be produced with an easily made scratch stock: Simply file a scrap piece of steel such as an old scraper blade or piece of bandsaw blade to

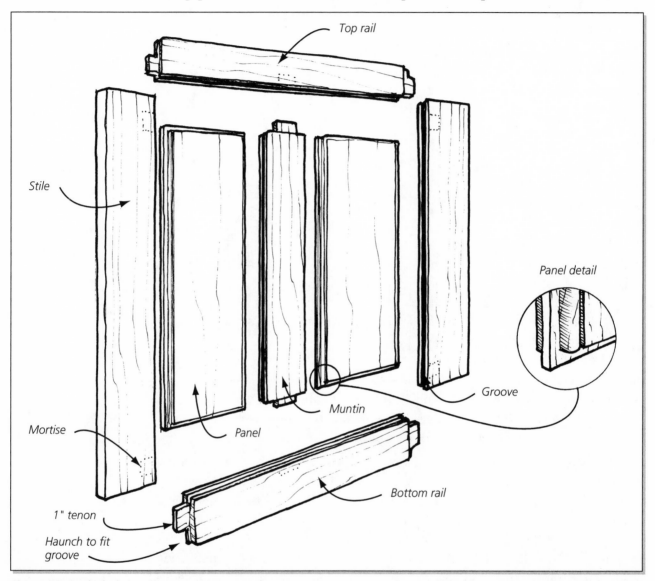

*Figure 60 Exploded
view of door and
back panel*

the desired shape, secure it in a stock and run it down the panel until the bead and quirk have been scratched out. It is also possible, of course, to use a router or shaper bit to produce the required profile, but this is a noisy and dusty way to proceed.

Clean the panels and framing members before assembly. Glue only the mortises and tenons, being careful that no excess glue escapes into the panel grooves, as the panels must remain free to float. After the frame is out of clamps, plane away any irregularities at the joints and trim the assembly to fit between the shelves, securing it with two countersunk screws through both shelves.

The door is made exactly the same way, except that when completed there should be ¹⁄₁₆ to ⅛ inch space all around so that it will open and shut easily. The door is hinged with a strip of piano-hinge along the entire width of its base. There

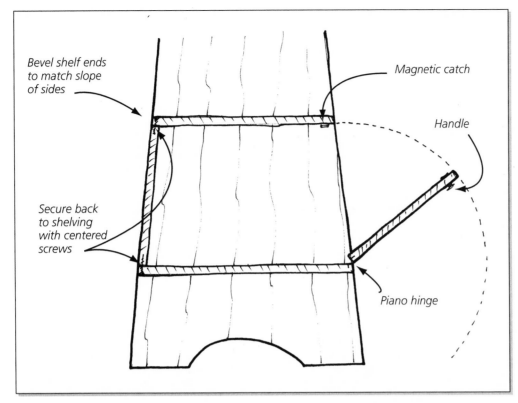

Bevel shelf ends to match slope of sides

Magnetic catch

Handle

Secure back to shelving with centered screws

Piano hinge

*Figure 61  Fitting back and door*

is no real need to mortise the hinge into the bottom of the door, but you may want to do this in the shelf for appearance' sake. Attach a simple handle at the top of the door, and adjust its closing by fixing a magnetic cabinet catch to the underside of the top shelf.

**Finishing and further possibilities**—All that remains is some final scraping or sanding and the application of any finish. The cherry had been hand-planed to perfection and required only a light, well-rubbed coat of oil. The pine was similarly treated before the entire unit was waxed. In time pine treated this way will darken to a very close match to the cherry. There is no reason why almost any other finish, or none at all, cannot be used. The only real considerations are how much sheen is desired and whether any protection against grubbiness is necessary.

Similarly, depending on the size of the cupboard and what you might store in it, some adjustable shelving might be provided. In keeping with the piece's knock-down character, this should also be made removable, perhaps resting on movable shelf supports inserted in a series of holes bored in the inside walls of the cupboard section.

2 sides ................................66″ x 20″ x 8¼″ x 1″

1 shelf ...............................19½″ x 18″ x 1″

1 shelf ...............................19½″ x 14½″ x 1″

1 shelf ...............................19½″ x 12″ x 1″

1 shelf ...............................19½″ x 11″ x 1″

1 shelf ...............................19½″ x 10″ x 1″

**Door and back panel:**

4 stiles ...............................18″ x 2¾″ x ¾″

2 bottom rails .........................14½″ x 3½″ x ¾″

2 top rails ............................14½″ x 2½″ x ¾″

2 muntins ............................15¼″ x 2″ x ¾″

4 panels ..............................14½″ x 5¾″ x ¾″

**Hardware:**

1 piano hinge .........................17″ x ½″

1 knob

1 magnetic catch

# Traveling trestle table

*Designing for convenience*

**F**urniture on the move—Six hundred years ago in Europe only the rich had furniture. Everyone else slept on the floor, sat around on crude benches, and generally led a life bereft of much that we would today consider essential furnishings. This state of affairs was not just the result of the general level of sophistication enjoyed by people in the fourteenth century, it was also due to relatively unstable social conditions. Even the rich were forced to carry their furniture around with them from castle to castle if they wanted to keep it in one piece. Such requirements had a strong influence on design. Many pieces were made to carry and store goods as well as provide seating, and most were made with portability in mind. This was the age of iron-bound chests and large box-chairs. Tables were no exception to the demands of the times, and a large and relatively immobile piece would have been out of the question. Consequently, collapsible units consisting of boards supported on removable trestles were very much the order of the day. Times are a little more secure now, but given the rate at which many people change address, an easily disassembled and transported table remains an idea whose day is far from over.

**Trestles old and new**—A trestle is essentially a support. In furniture the trestle is understood as a pair of diverging legs, joined at their upper end, and commonly used to support a table or bench. They are usually used in pairs and are frequently capable of being folded up and easily moved. But a trestle may have other forms. So long as it retains the ability to support a superincumbent structure, it remains a trestle. The trestle design used in the traveling table actually consists of three pieces: two uprights and a connecting horizontal beam. The beam is, in fact, the piece originally meant by the word "trestle"; it derives from the Latin *transtellum,* meaning something "placed across."

Despite the general interpretation of the word "trestle," the term "trestle table" most often implies something slightly different: a table that is not supported by either a single central column or pedestal or the conventional four corner legs. Many such contemporary trestle tables, however, are also not collapsible, hence the need to distinguish this particular table, which is remarkably easy to dismantle, transport, and reassemble.

**The traveling trestle**—I have made several of these tables, each one slightly different from its predecessor, but all with the same basic framework. The first one was designed in response to the problem of how to build a table larger than could be negotiated up stairways and through doors that were too small to admit the finished piece to its intended location. Subsequent ones were made in a similar fashion purely to take advantage of the ease of transporting a piece of furniture that is readily dismantled into conveniently small pieces. This is still, however, a substantial piece of furniture which when assembled is rock steady and gives no impression of impermanence. It is not the same as a folding card table or a picnic table, the very essence of which is their temporary nature and almost instant erection, for it takes half an hour or so to take apart and reassemble each time. Nevertheless, unlike more monolithic structures, it is possible to move this piece in a medium-size automobile if necessary.

*Figure 62  How character of boards may determine shape of top*

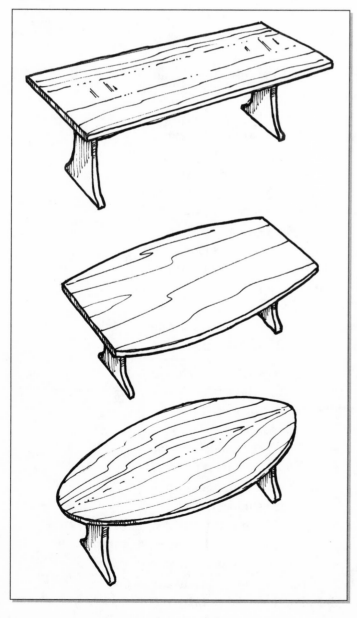

**Size and dimensional considerations**—Because this table comes apart, it can also be thought of as modular, and as such is capable of being built with differently sized parts to fit different areas. The same trestle can be used to support tops of different sizes, and even parts of the trestle can be built to different measurements depending on your needs. The measurements given here may be thought of as resulting in the standard model, but there is no reason why, when the structure is understood, you can't build it to different dimensions. As a table it is, of course, subject to certain limitations: The top should be about 29 inches high if it is to be used for writing, and lower still if a typewriter or keyboard is to be accommodated. If its main function is as a dining table, 30 inches will be a better height. Any construction attached to the underside of the top should allow sufficient knee room for someone sitting on an average 18-inch-high chair, which means a lower limit of around 24 inches. And the width of the top, if intended as a dining table for facing diners, should be at least 30 inches. Each use will dictate its own set of dimensions, as will the requirements and physical size of the owner.

If you bear all this in mind, making sure you understand the minimum requirements of the individual structural components, and remain flexible, it will be perfectly all right to change any of the dimensions given here. I have rarely made two pieces with identical dimensions except, of course, when building sets of chairs or purposely matching units. The top of this table, for example, as finished is 76⅛ inches long by 31⅜ inches wide, although the original intention was for something 76 inches by 32 inches. The slight variations are of little importance and result from other considerations that occurred during construction.

**The top**—In lieu of other requirements, the top is often a good place to start, as it is the most visible. It is also the part most easily varied. A straight-sided top can have advantages if the piece is to be placed against a wall, but there is no reason why some other shape might not be used (*Figure 62*). All other things being equal, let the material decide the size and shape. The boards I had available for the top of the traveling trestle table, three particularly nice pieces of mahogany, were long enough, but when joined didn't give me the required width. It was an easy matter to rip an 8-inch piece of padauk into two 3½-inch boards and thereby increase the width and add a little extra complementary color to the design.

The actual process is an exercise in careful jointing. All five constituent boards are simply butt-jointed; no splines, pins, biscuits, or tongues and grooves are necessary if the stock is prepared carefully. Jointers and planers can save a lot of handwork when preparing perfectly flat and equally thicknessed boards, as well as then obtaining perfectly square and true edges, but surfacing can also be done by hand if you are equipped with properly conditioned planes and winding sticks. So far as surface preparation is concerned, it is often safer to use hand planes when dealing with figured or cross-grained material—this avoids the dreaded tear-out often encountered with powertools.

When the boards to be joined are all of the same thickness and are perfectly flat, with no winding, twisting, or cupping, prepare their edges for butt-jointing. To do this successfully, and without having to depend on splines or pins or clamps to pull the boards together in perfect alignment, requires that the edges be shot perfectly square and true. Very careful use of an exactly adjusted power jointer will achieve this, but more control is possible by using a plane. The ideal tool is the longest try plane or jointer you have, used in conjunction with a machinist's straightedge. A machinist's straightedge is a precision instrument. If, when placed on the top of the edge, it does not rock or show any light between it and the wood, it will show that the edge is flat enough for a perfect butt joint—provided it is also square.

*Figure 63 Correcting squareness*

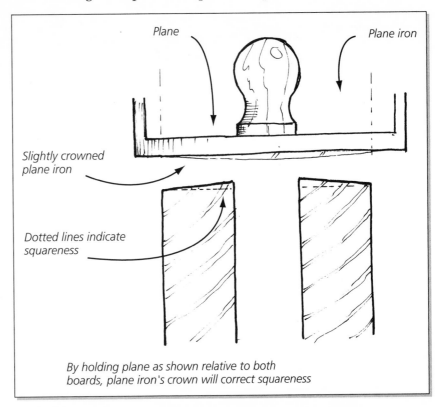

Plane

Plane iron

Slightly crowned plane iron

Dotted lines indicate squareness

*By holding plane as shown relative to both boards, plane iron's crown will correct squareness*

To joint an edge by hand takes a little practice, but when the skill is acquired you have more control over the vagaries of grain and density. The plane iron should be very sharp, ground with the merest crown, and set with the smallest possible mouth so that if one side of the edge is too high, planing with the tool off center will produce the required uneven shaving (*Figure 63*). Use the straight-edge and the trysquare frequently and make every inch of every pass count. When adjacent edges have been prepared as perfectly as possible this way, proceed by testing the fit with the boards themselves, adjusting with the plane by taking the slightest shavings possible. The aim should be two edges that fit so well together that they almost create a suction effect when you attempt to separate them. Such joints need only to be coated with glue and lightly clamped to form joints stronger than the wood itself.

When the entire top has been thus assembled, both the underside and the top should be planed clean. The best finished surface will then be obtained if you use a well-tuned smooth plane rather than abrading and filling the grain with dust by the use of sandpaper. If the grain is too difficult to manage by hand, a scraper may help, but this also needs to be extremely sharp.

I had originally planned on a top 1 inch thick, but by the time I reached this stage the actual thickness was slightly less than ⅞ inch. To give the top a fatter look, I finished the edges with an upward-facing bevel. If the top had been too thick, a downward-facing bevel would have achieved the opposite effect, making it appear thinner. If the top is just right, consider other edge treatments from perfectly square to rounded over or moulded into quarter-rounds, thumbnails, or ogees (*Figure 64*). Moulding such a large piece is most easily done by hand, using a plane with an angle guide or a specific moulding plane. An electric router is another choice, but take extreme care not to chip away the corners, burn the surface, or slip. Furthermore, when you've finished you still have to clean up the surface to remove the cutter marks, whereas the surface left by a plane is one facet, already partly burnished by the plane's wooden sole.

**The trestle ends**—The trestle consists of two ends, a crossbar held in the ends by removable wedges, and a substructure that connects the tops of the two ends. This substructure is in the form of a shallow framework holding three drawers. The drawers can be omitted (although they are useful for holding cutlery and table linen if the table is to be used for dining, or pens and pencils if the table is to be used as a writing desk), but the basic framework of the substructure

*Figure 64  Edge profiles*

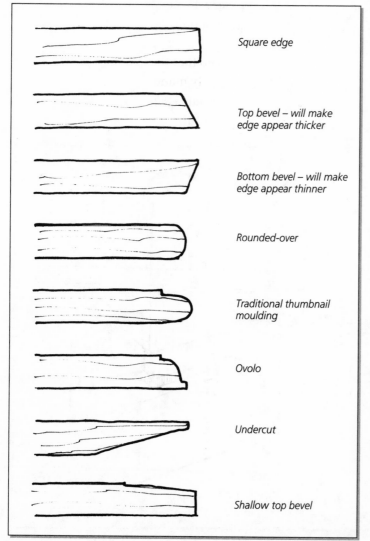

Square edge

Top bevel – will make edge appear thicker

Bottom bevel – will make edge appear thinner

Rounded-over

Traditional thumbnail moulding

Ovolo

Undercut

Shallow top bevel

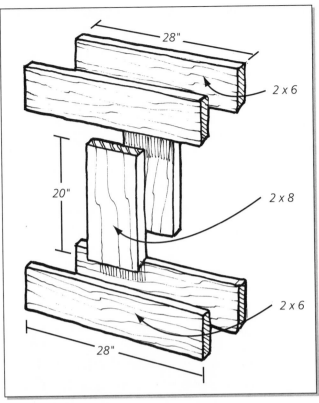

is the key to the table's integrity and rigidity when assembled.

Make the ends first. Each end consists of three pieces: a top, a bottom crosspiece, and a vertical piece (*Figure 65*). The vertical pieces are 20 inches long, and can be prepared from two-by-eight material. The horizontal crosspieces are 28 inches long but may be prepared from two-by-six material. The idea is to make the top horizontal piece a couple of inches or so shorter than the width of the top, thereby providing the maximum amount of support necessary to keep the top flat. Whatever the width of this top piece, the bottom piece should be about an inch or so wider to preserve the proportions of the ends.

All three pieces are first prepared to thickness and left rectilinear so that the mortise-and-tenon joints (*Figure 66*) that connect them may be more easily made. After assembling both ends, trace the actual shape required from a template (*Figure 67*) made of cardboard, masonite, or even stiff paper. I make these full-size patterns for any curved work I do and, carefully labeling them, keep them for possible future use. Nevertheless, refinement is always possible, and indeed is sometimes demanded by the presence of a knot or some other peculiarity of the material.

The traced outline should then be cut with bow saw or bandsaw, the resultant surfaces and curves smoothed with files and spokeshaves, and all arrises rounded over except those that will abut the underneath of the top and those that will rest on the floor. This final rounding over, which should produce a curve equal to a quarter of a circle measuring about an inch or so in diameter, is one place where careful use of an electric router fitted with a sharp round-over bit may prove easier than working with traditional handtools. Take care to pre-

*Figure 65  Parts
needed for the ends*

*Figure 66  Stub
mortise-and-tenon
dimensions*

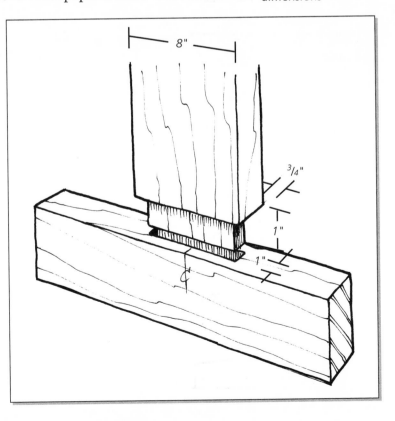

serve the shape of the inside curves and watch the direction of the bit when working the corners.

**The crossbar**—Prepare the crossbar from a single piece, 2 inches wide by 3 inches deep and 59 inches long. Both ends of the crossbar are then reduced to 1¼ inches by 2 inches for a distance of 4 inches (*Figure 68*). Cut corresponding through-mortises in each of the end pieces, assemble crossbar and ends, and mark the location of the wedge mortises in the ends of the crossbar.

This is all straightforward work, but a few tips are worth bearing in mind: First, the location of the mortises in the end pieces must be carefully considered. If they are too low, they are liable to get in the way of your feet when sitting at the table; too high, and it will be uncomfortable to rest your feet on them. The lower the crossbar, the greater strength it provides, but you do not want to weaken the joints connecting the upright and bottom parts of the ends, so the position as shown, just above the joint, is perhaps ideal.

Second, it is likely to have proved easier to mark out these mortises while the ends were still rectilinear, before they were sawed to shape, but in any event work first from the outside of each end since the inside face will be partly covered by the shoulders of the tenon on the crossbar, and any slight misalignment can be hidden. It is bad practice to make allowances in advance like this for expected errors; you should anticipate and strive for exactness at all parts of the job. At the same time, however, a little insurance is always prudent!

Third, bevel the ends of the tenon and the edges of the mortise on the inside face of the ends so that there is less risk of splitting out the edges of the mortise every time the crossbar is removed and replaced.

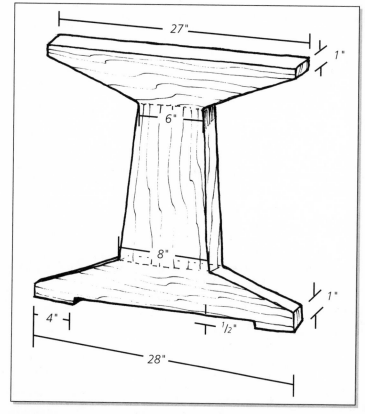

*Figure 67
Completed end
dimensions before
edge rounding*

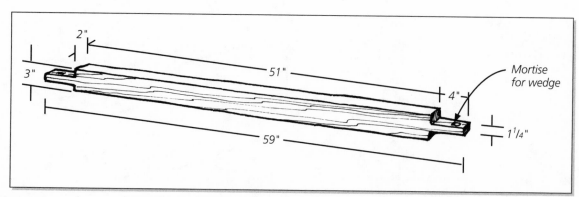

*Figure 68  Crossbar
dimensions*

Last, make sure that the inside face of the wedge mortise is positioned a little *inside* the outside face of the ends (*Figure 69*). It is better thus to create a slight draw-bored effect than to cut this mortise so that no matter how firmly the wedge is pushed in, it can never make contact with the outside face of the end.

**Crossbar wedges**—The wedges, also known as keys, that hold the crossbar to the ends are best made of something somewhat harder than the rest of the table. It is preferable for the ends to be slightly deformed by the wedges than to allow the wedges themselves to become deformed. Their shape is critical. If the angle is too steep, the wedges will be inclined to work loose; if the angle is too shallow, it will be difficult to remove them. Therefore cut the wedges with a slope on the outside face only at a pitch approximately 1 in 13.

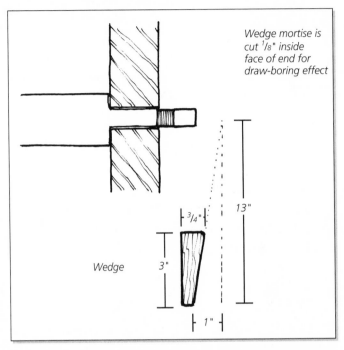

**The substructure framework**—When the lower part of the trestle assembly is complete, make the top part—the substructure—to match. The outside length of the substructure must equal the distance between the tenon shoulders on the crossbeam, which should have been 51 inches. If there was any variation, adjust the length of the substructure accordingly.

A shallow framework is required, no more than 3 inches deep, that fits between the ends and is somewhat less than the width of the top. Centered across the length of the top is a 3-inch-wide member that overlaps the framework and is cut to the shape of a dovetail at each end. These dovetail ends drop into matching mortises cut in the top of the end pieces. Together with screws inserted into the end pieces from the inside of the framework's ends, this dovetailed center member holds the end pieces together at the top in the same way that the crossbar holds them together near their bottom.

*Figure 69  Cross-section of crossbar and end and wedge dimensions*

*Figure 70  Simple framework without drawers*

In addition to being fixed through slot-screw mortises in the upper parts of the end pieces (as described a little further on), the tabletop is also secured by three screws inserted through this central member. This procedure has the added advantage of ensuring that the substructure itself cannot sag should it be fitted with heavily loaded drawers.

If drawers are to be fitted, proceed as directed below, but should you elect not to include drawers, just construct a simple framework (*Figure 70*), making sure to leave access to those parts through which screws are to be inserted into the end pieces and the top.

**Substructure with drawers**—The traveling trestle table as illustrated has three drawers that fit flush with the front of the framework. They are care-

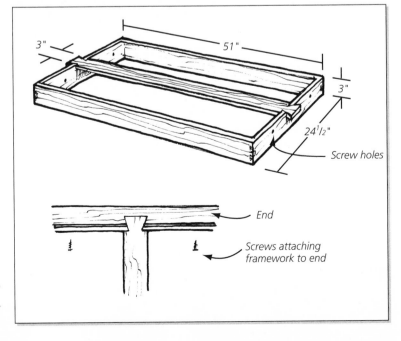

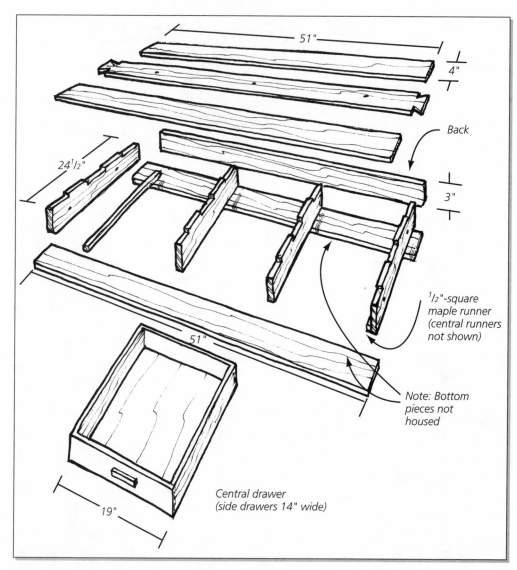

51"

4"

*Back*

24¹/₂"

3"

¹/₂"-square
maple runner
(central runners
not shown)

51"

*Note: Bottom
pieces not
housed*

19"

*Central drawer
(side drawers 14" wide)*

*Figure 71
Substructure and
drawer dimensions*

fully made to slide on small runners fixed to the sides of the four main front-to-back members of the substructure. Make these four pieces first to the dimensions shown in *Figure 71*, and then cut housings in the center of each to accommodate the central member so that it can be fitted flush with their top surface. Four pieces 51 inches long and measuring at least ¼ inch thick by 4 inches wide are now secured by gluing and screwing to the front and back top and bottom edges of the crosspieces. Note that the top pieces should be housed similarly to the central member, but that this is not necessary for the two bottom pieces.

The central member, as explained above, is longer than the four pieces just made in order that shallow but wide dovetails can be cut at each overlapping end. These should be no more than 1¾ inches deep so that they do not show through the end pieces. Mark their corresponding mortises directly from the dovetails and you will be assured of a perfect fit even if the dovetails have been cut a little irregularly. By doing so purposely, you make it easier to see which end piece goes at the left or right end of the table; in any event, stamp matching numbers on all adjoining parts so that the various parts of the trestle can always be reassembled in the same order and relation.

At the rear of the framework, fix a single piece to cover the backs of the drawer compartments so that when viewed from this side the table will appear to have a normal skirt. If this side is to be visible, joining the skirt to the ends of the framework with lapped dovetails is a nice touch, although merely gluing is sufficiently strong.

Standard dovetailed drawers should be made to fit in flush with the ends of the cross members, to which small runners made of ½-inch-square maple or some other hardwood should be fitted, flush with their bottom edges.

If the drawers are made somewhat shorter than the width of the substructure as measured from front to back, you can create a usable secret compartment between the back of the drawer and the skirt mentioned above which will be accessible from underneath the table.

**Fixing the top**—Assemble the trestle as follows: First, fix the crossbar to the ends and lightly drop the wedges into place. Next, drop the substructure into place so that the dovetails engage. Then screw through the ends of the substructure into the end pieces, taking care that the tops of the substructure's ends remain perfectly flush with the tops of the end pieces. In order that these screws do not interfere with the smooth operation of the drawers, they should be carefully countersunk below the surface. When the substructure is thus brought snugly up against the end pieces, tap the crossbar wedges in more firmly. The trestle should now comprise a solid unit.

Turn this unit upside down and bore slot-screw mortises into the bottoms of the end pieces' tops (*Figure 72*). Also prepare countersunk pilot holes for the screws that will hold the cross member tightly to the underside of the tabletop.

The attaching of the top is most easily accomplished with the entire piece the

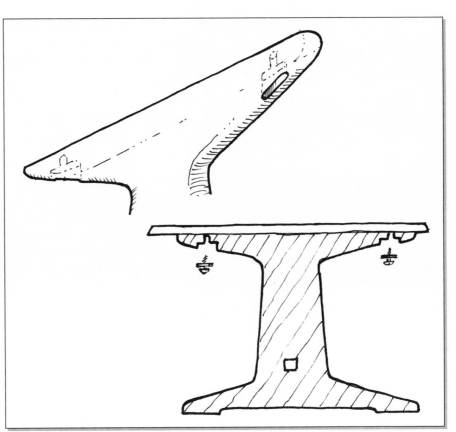

*Figure 72 Slot-screwing top*

right way up; the only difficulty is in positioning the top exactly over the trestle. To do this, take frequent measurements from various points around the top's circumference to the ends of the trestles, and when you are satisfied, clamp the top to the substructure before starting to screw. Subsequent assemblies will be merely a matter of aligning the screw holes in the top with the slot-screw mortises and the pilot holes in the central member. This process is made considerably easier if strong light is available.

**Details**—I have said little about such details as fitting partitions in the drawers, their actual construction, and the kinds of handles used, and nothing about the carving visible on the ends; all this is up to the individual. Drawer-making is a subject in itself, but what material to use for the drawer fronts and their handles—in this case amaranth and ebony, respectively—is largely a question of personal design preferences. I chose the amaranth since it matched the mahogany's intensity well and provided a dramatic contrast to the dovetailed white maple sides of the drawers. The ebony is especially beautiful against the purple amaranth, and used in such small pieces provided a visual connection with the ebony wedges holding the crossbar to the ends.

Finishing was accomplished with a danish oil. Many extremely light coats were applied twenty-four hours apart. Seven or more coats applied like this will provide a finish that stands up well to dining-table use, including spills of water and alcohol, and although there is often a rush to get the finished piece out of the shop, there is less actual work involved than there is in flooding the surface for twenty minutes and then wiping up the excess, as is sometimes recommended. This wiping is very hard to do and the invariable result, especially on mahogany, is a daily recurrence of new fish-eyed spots of oil leaking out onto the surface. It is true that they are easily dissolved by a fresh application of the oil, but it is all too easy to miss some here and there; I find it easier to apply coats of oil so lightly that it is only just possible to see the smear of fresh oil as you wipe the rag over the piece.

Finish the table disassembled so that all parts and surfaces are equally treated. When done, apply a wax finish to the tenons of the crossbar to make assembly easy.

## CUTTING LIST

1 top . . . . . . . . . . . . . . . . . . . . . . . . . . . . . . . . . 76⅛″ x 31⅜″ x ⅞″

**Legs:**
2 top pieces . . . . . . . . . . . . . . . . . . . . . . . . . . 28″ x 2″ x 6″
2 bottom pieces . . . . . . . . . . . . . . . . . . . . . . . . 28″ x 2″ x 6″
2 vertical pieces . . . . . . . . . . . . . . . . . . . . . . . 20″ x 2″ x 8″ x 6″
1 crossbar . . . . . . . . . . . . . . . . . . . . . . . . . . . 59″ x 3″ x 2″
2 wedges . . . . . . . . . . . . . . . . . . . . . . . . . . . . . 3″ x ¾″ x ¾″

**Substructure:**
1 back . . . . . . . . . . . . . . . . . . . . . . . . . . . . . . . 51″ x 3″ x ¾″
1 front . . . . . . . . . . . . . . . . . . . . . . . . . . . . . . . 51″ x 3″ x ¾″
1 centerpiece . . . . . . . . . . . . . . . . . . . . . . . . . . 53″ x 3″ x ¾″
2 ends . . . . . . . . . . . . . . . . . . . . . . . . . . . . . . . 24½″ x 3″ x ¾″

**Hardware:**
4 #8 x 2½-inch roundhead screws
4 ½-inch flat washers

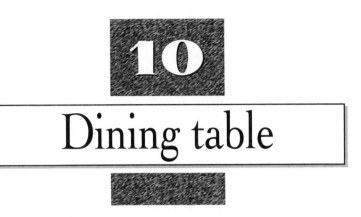

# Dining table

*Unusual requirements*

Your job as a designer will sometimes require you to work out solutions that cannot be found in standard texts on woodworking or that are not duplicated in project books. This project is an example of how to accommodate unusual requirements that may require new ways to effect them, and how to get the most advantage out of what may at first seem like problematical limitations. Part of the design as finally realized—namely the substructure—calls for fairly standard construction and is described only summarily. The only unusual feature, represented by the curved skirt, is actually a straightforward procedure. This chapter concentrates on the solution to the design problem and the technique developed for constructing the solid banding.

The initial problem is how to design a table big enough for the occasional dinner party of twelve or so people, but that does not dwarf the three or four people who use it the rest of the time. A table that expands and contracts by means of sliding, removable, or folding leaves is out of the question because in its contracted state it looks too small for the room it must occupy.

The solution is a large table with removable ends which when not required for the maximum number of diners stand separately against the wall. Such an arrangement leaves a smaller, more intimate table for three or four, and yet still fills the room comfortably.

The removable sections are designed with semicircular tops which become pier tables when placed against a wall. When used together they form a single round table. When situated at either end of the main rectangular part, the whole assumes the form known as a racetrack table. Besides maintaining comfortable spatial relationships between the room and the table, this arrangement also makes possible a variety of seating opportunities (*Figure 73*).

**Construction**—The skirts and legs, which are made after the top is completed, present few problems, but the top is considerably more involved. Its construction is detailed below.

The tabletop is edged in solid wood, but the central areas are veneered. Not only does veneer make the construction of a large flat surface easier than with solid wood, but it also allows the use of a patterned figure and, most importantly in this case, avoids the problems of expansion and contraction that a solid surface might have on a semicircular solid banding.

Banding, circular or straight, is frequently veneered cross-grain onto solid or other laminated stock. This has its advantages: the grain is always perpendicular to the edge; there is little waste; and the pieces used are often small enough to minimize any wood-movement problems. Solid banding, on the other hand, also has advantages: the edge does not have to be separately veneered or previously faced, and it is easier to work any desired moulding in a solid edge rather than in a veneered or composite edge.

If you veneer a surface all of whose edges you intend to band, it is easiest to make an oversized panel and trim it to size after the veneer has been applied. In this case, since there is no banding on the straight sides of the semicircular ends and no banding on the matching ends of the rectangular center section (in order that the completely assembled table will present an unbroken veneered surface), the edges of the core that are not to be banded are first faced with a ½-inch-wide plain edging of solid maple. The alternative would have been to veneer the edge after the panel had been laid up and trimmed. There is nothing wrong with this procedure except that it results in an additional line of veneer (*Figure 74*).

*Figure 73 Seating opportunities*

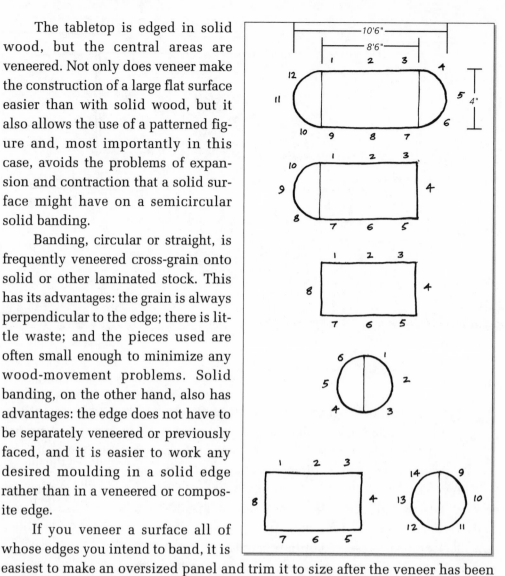

*Figure 74*

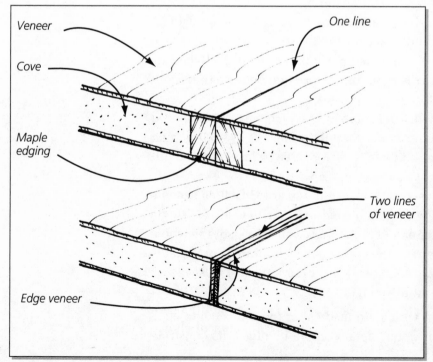

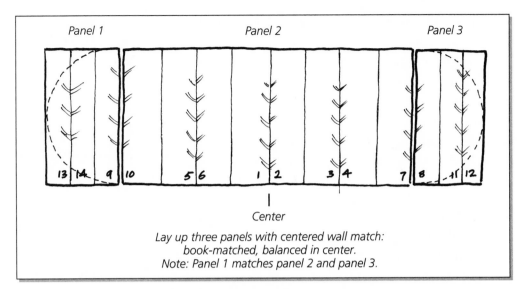

Panel 1    Panel 2    Panel 3

13 14  9 10    5 6    1 2    3 4    7 8  11 12

Center

Lay up three panels with centered wall match:
book-matched, balanced in center.
Note: Panel 1 matches panel 2 and panel 3.

Figure 75 Veneer
layout

Fiddleback maple is laid up in a center wall-match pattern onto a substrate of standard density particleboard (*Figure 75*). This pattern ensures that the two end sections will join the center section and each other with a book-match that is balanced from the very center of the table. The bottom surface is simply slip-matched with plain maple. The pattern here is not important since the underside of the table is not normally visible, but it is extremely important to veneer both sides of any panel to equalize moisture content changes.

**Cutting the semicircular ends**—Make sure that the mating edges of the two ends do, in fact, mate perfectly, align the veneer, and establish the center of the matching edge. As a precautionary measure, first describe the desired semicircle on the panel using a pair of trammel points with a pencil attachment. Mount the router in a simple circle-cutting jig and position the jig on each panel in turn at the center mark, set to cut ⅛ inch outside the pencil line. Make several increasingly deep passes with a ½-inch double-flute up-cut bit to cut out the semicircle. Bring the panel to size and leave a perfectly square cut by running the router around the semicircle the "wrong" way with a light finishing cut.

**Making the banding**—The center section is banded with two straight pieces cut to the same width as the trimmed banding on the semicircular ends, straightforwardly splined in stopped grooves and glued up. Banding the ends is considerably more involved.

The number of segments needed is a matter of how well you can match the grain, but for a two-part circular top the number must necessarily be even. Twelve produces a conveniently sized piece. Find the circumference using the formula $2\pi R$, where $\pi$ equals 3.1416 and $R$ equals the radius of the circle. Choose a board about ¹⁄₁₆ inch thicker than the top and somewhat longer than the circumference and mark the required number of segments sequentially so that the grain will match from segment to segment. Being able to lay out a couple of extra segments is good insurance.

Make a template for the segments by marking off around one of the semicircles the position of each of the six segments. The distance between marks will give you the inside measurement of the segment, and you can trace the inside curve directly from the panel. The width of the banding is a matter of choice; 3 inches was used for the table illustrated here.

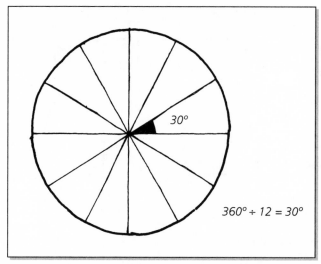

*Figure 76  Twelve-
segmented circle*

Dividing a circle into twelve parts is a simple geometric exercise that can be done with a compass or arithmetically, simply dividing 360° by 12. The resulting angle at the center of the circle made by each of the twelve pie-shaped segments is 30° (*Figure 76*).

Produce these lines to the circumference and measure carefully between each point. The distance between each pair must be equal. If necessary, average unequal distances and mark and measure again until each segment is exactly the same length.

In order to make clamping and final trimming as easy as possible, cut the segments from a board that is the same width throughout its length. This will also

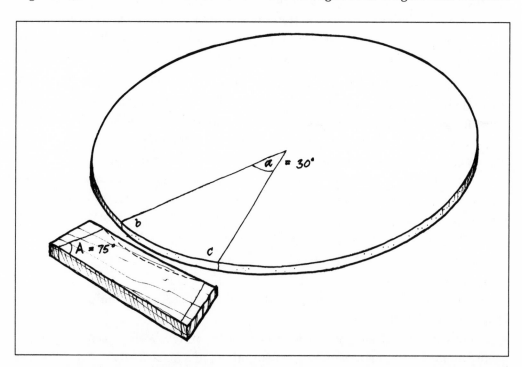

*Figure 77  Laying out
template*

make cutting the angled abutting edges of the segments simple. *Figure 77* shows that what you need to know in order to be able to cut out a template (and segment) is angle *A*. Since angle *a* has already been found to be 30°, angle *b* plus angle *c* must equal 150° since there are only 180° in a triangle. If the board has parallel sides, angle *b*, which is half *a* plus *b* (since the triangle is isosceles) must equal angle *A*, that is, 75°.

This completes the information needed to make the template for laying out the segments on the board. Keep the segments marked so that you do not confuse their order.

Cut the miters at exactly 75° and so that the distance on the short side is *exactly* the same as the distance between the marks on the circumference of the top. This is essential if the segments are to join perfectly and completely encircle the top. The next step is to cut the inside curve of the segments to fit the curve of the top. The hand method involves tracing the required curve directly from the top onto the segments and sawing to the line, smoothing the cut with a circular plane. Using a simple circle-cutting jig on a tablesaw properly set up reduces the labor considerably.

The tablesaw method requires that the table, jig, and segment all be perfectly perpendicular to the bandsaw blade, or the segments will tilt when joined to the top. Second, for a perfect arc the leading edge of the teeth must be exactly perpendicular to the exact center of the jig's pivot point. Third, the distance between the center of the pivot point and the inside edge of the blade must be the same as the radius of the tabletop.

Before cutting the spline grooves in the segments, lay them around the top to check how well they fit, adjusting as necessary. Remember that if they seem a trifle large, clamping will probably make them fit perfectly. Cut the grooves with a slotting bit in the router. Make sure the bit is the same thickness as the splines you intend to use. If the segments have indeed been cut from stock that is ⅟₁₆ inch thicker than the top, cut the groove in the table edge first, then lower the bit ⅟₃₂ inch before cutting the grooves in the segments. This centers the segments on the top, leaving them slightly proud for easier planing and cleaning up when attached.

To prevent the splines from showing, stop the router before reaching the ends of the semicircular tops and similarly before reaching the ends of those segments that will lie at these points. Additionally, stop the groove that is cut in the mitered sections of the segments before it reaches what will be the outside radius of the banding (*Figure 78*).

You can make the splines from a variety of materials. If you use wood, make sure the grain is at right angles to the length of the spline. This will involve so many pieces that you may prefer to use a material like masonite or thin plywood. A 3-inch-wide banding can be held securely with a spline measuring 1 inch wide. Lay out sufficient strips using trammel points set ½ inch farther apart than for the radius of the veneered section of the top. Bandsaw to these lines, use a marking gauge set to 1 inch to mark lines parallel to the inside radius of the spline, and then bandsaw to these lines (*Figure 79*).

Cut a little more spline than needed to completely encircle the top so that there will be enough to lay out in such a way that spline joints avoid the segment joints. Cut the splines joining the segments' miters from a single straight section,

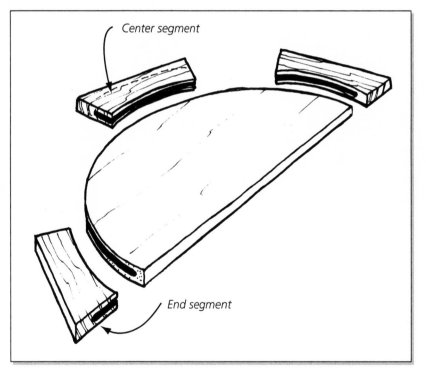

*Figure 78 Stopped grooves*

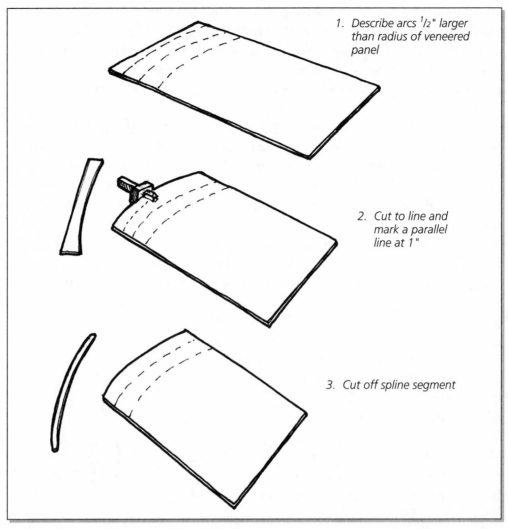

1. Describe arcs ¹/₂" larger than radius of veneered panel

2. Cut to line and mark a parallel line at 1"

3. Cut off spline segment

*Figure 79
Making splines*

rounding their ends to fit the rounded end of the slot (*Figure 80*). Before gluing up, check that the spline is nowhere too wide.

**Assembly**—First glue the edge spline into one of the semicircular tops, then glue the first end segment and attach it. Glue and insert the miter spline and attach the next segment, and so on, until both halves are banded. Clamp both halves together with a band clamp, pulling together opposite pairs of segments where necessary with bar, sash, or pipe clamps.

*Figure 80 Miter
spline segments*

To ensure that the end segments on both halves line up with the ends of the halves, insert a waxed strip of batten between the two halves and make adjustments with shims. Gluing up a 4-foot-diameter top is a lot of work. White glue will give you a little more working time than will

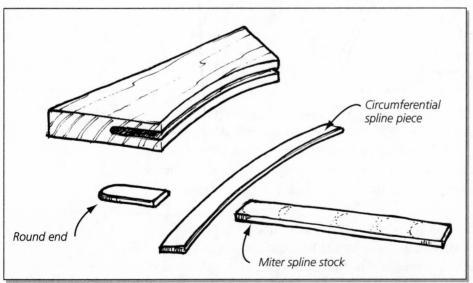

Circumferential spline piece

Round end

Miter spline stock

yellow glue, but you still must work fast. Position each segment exactly for it will not want to move horizontally when its neighbors are in place.

As soon as you're sure that all segments are tight against the veneered panels and that all miters are closed, make a final circuit before the final tightening of the band clamp to check that each segment is flush with its neighbor. Any discrepancy here can be fixed with a smaller clamp placed directly over the joint.

After the glue has set, remove the clamps, separate the two halves, and reattach the router circle-cutting jig, increasing the radius by 3 inches. Working in small increments to avoid tear-out, trim the dodecagonal top to a circle.

Final treatment of the edge can be accomplished by further routing or a few passes of a finely set circular plane. Plane the top and bottom surfaces flush with the veneer before a final scraping of the entire top.

**The substructure**—Cut the legs to size but leave them square to facilitate the mortising necessary to receive the skirts. Make the skirting for the semicircular ends from ⅛-inch-thick strips glued together around a plywood form cut to the correct radius.

Attach the two central legs at each end with bridle joints. Attach the others with mitered blind mortise-and-tenons (*Figure 81*).

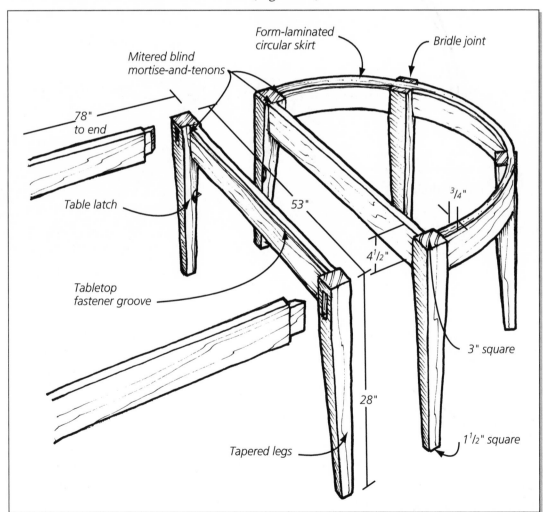

Form-laminated circular skirt

Bridle joint

Mitered blind mortise-and-tenons

78" to end

Table latch

53"

¾"

4½"

Tabletop fastener groove

3" square

28"

Tapered legs

1½" square

Before gluing the skirts to the legs, slot the top inside edge of the skirts to receive the buttons or tabletop fasteners which will secure the top, and taper the legs.

*Figure 81 Substructure details*

**Tops** (inclusive of banding):

1 center . . . . . . . . . . . . . . . . . . . . . . . . . . . . . . .78″ x 55″ x 1″

2 ends . . . . . . . . . . . . . . . . . . . . . . . . . . . . . .55″ x 54-inch radius x 1″

8 legs . . . . . . . . . . . . . . . . . . . . . . . . . . . . . .28″ x 3-inches square x
1½-inches square

**Skirts:**

2 long . . . . . . . . . . . . . . . . . . . . . . . . . . . . . .75″ x 4½″ x ¾″

2 short . . . . . . . . . . . . . . . . . . . . . . . . . . . . . .50″ x 4½″ x ¾″

2 semicircular . . . . . . . . . . . . . . . . . . . . . . . . .54-inch radius x 4½″ x ¾″

**Hardware:**
  4  table latches
 16  tabletop fasteners
  8  furniture glides

# Standing cabinet

*Contemporary design*

Mention was made at the start of chapter 6 of the difficulty of "reinventing the wheel" and at the same time of how central to the human character is the need to create something new. Designing furniture is an ideal field for this endeavor. Once the utilitarian and constructional aspects that have been stressed in previous chapters have been thoroughly understood, there remains the purely aesthetic side. It is not that this part of the equation can be regarded apart from the other more pedestrian concerns but that it should play an equally important part if the design is to have any artistic merit.

Never forgetting the lessons of the earlier chapters, you should simultaneously be aware of the aesthetic impact of the design. This simply means paying attention to how the piece looks. Although largely subjective and dependent on the degree of sophistication possessed by the observer, certain things are quite straightforward and easily seen once you look for them. Is the piece balanced or does it look top-heavy or about to fall over? Does it complement its surroundings or does it somehow stand out as jarringly inappropriate—is it the wrong color or the wrong shape? Is it perhaps built in a style so different from other pieces nearby that it seems out of place? This last consideration is often one of the first things to determine a design. Style is infinite and need not be controlled by the need to match existing styles. That a piece's style *complement* its surroundings is more useful an idea than that it necessarily be a member of the same club. It is, however, somewhat easier, especially if you feel a little unsure of whether something will fit in, to design in a similar style.

The standing cabinet is clearly contemporary in that it lacks any characteristics easily identifiable with previous stylistic periods. It has no mouldings common to furniture of the sixteenth-century oak period (as shown it isn't even made of oak, although there is no reason why you might not use oak to build it) and it has none of the characteristics of seventeenth- and early eighteenth-century walnut furniture even though walnut is used and it lacks any of the many features by which we identify furniture variously classified as Sheraton, Hepplewhite, Federal, etc. Notwithstanding the fact that so-called contemporary furniture may indeed belong quite definitely to any one of a number of distinct style schools ranging from the tonally quiet and homogenous pieces most often thought of in connection with contemporary woodworkers such as James Krenov and Sam Maloof, to the loud and striking designs of the Memphis School, or the more visceral, sculptural creations of Michael Coffey and Wendel Castle, the standing cabinet remains squarely contemporary by virtue of its reliance upon relatively plain, unadorned volumes to constitute its superficial design.

You may choose to build it from different woods and in so doing alter its color to something whose effect is either louder, and more glaring or to something even quieter and more subdued. Using a soft, fine-grained material such as pear or ash or elm would produce the latter effect. Choosing highly figured and contrasting woods for its different parts would produce a startlingly different effect. But in either case, the piece's predominant presence is a result of its strictly rectangular form.

*Figure 82 Standing cabinet dimensions*

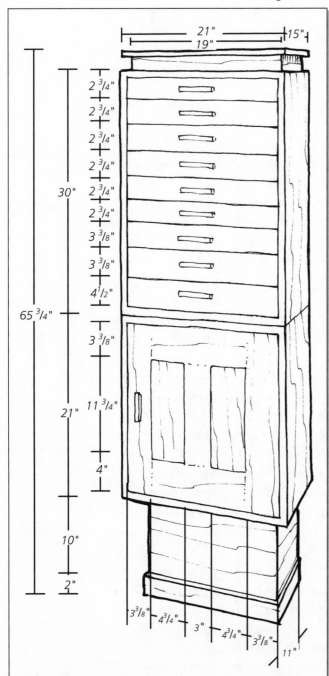

**Design considerations**—Although strictly rectilinear and simple in form, the standing cabinet is constructed using a variety of joints including mortise-and-tenon, several types of dovetail, splined miters, and mitered clamp joints. Despite the sophistication of the construction, the shape is the chief design element. It is contemporary in feeling, consisting of massed volumes unadorned by any moulding, carving, or surface decoration. It is the relationship of the various parts, in terms of both shape and color, that gives the piece interest (*Figure 82*).

It was designed specifically as a silver cabinet, the drawers being intended to hold cutlery and the cupboard below them to hold plate. It could serve a number of other purposes equally well: a carving cabinet, with the drawers fitted out to hold chisels and gouges and the cupboard forming the ideal place to keep mallets and clamps; a music cabinet, the shallow drawers being well suited for sheet music; or a collector's cabinet for anything from coins to butterflies. Its modular construction is an additional advantage since it can be easily disassembled and transported.

While there are no real structural reasons why the relative sizes and spacings of the various parts such as drawers and cupboard section could not be altered, care should be taken to preserve overall harmonious proportions. This is largely subjective but should be considered carefully before function is allowed to dictate radical changes.

**Choice of material**—Although the contrasting woods of the cabinet as built constitute much of its appeal, the same design might be duplicated using other species, or even a single species. Certain species are inappropriate, such as softwoods for drawer runners, but very often the choice of material starts from a particular given. In this case, I had long been saving a wonderful board of rare Brazilian rosewood, which I realized would be just enough to make the drawer fronts and the door frame. When I also acquired a few pieces of amaranth that complemented the rosewood, the project became a reality.

Starting with rosewood and amaranth led to the choice of walnut for the carcase, because its color was sympathetic and allowed the rosewood to dominate. Maple was used for the drawer sides; the contrast was dramatic when the drawers were opened, showing off the dovetailing to advantage, and, more important, hard-wearing maple is an excellent structural choice for side-hung drawers.

Wood that is not normally seen, such as the bottoms, backs, and interior sections of a piece, is often referred to as secondary wood, and is usually less fancy and expensive than is the primary species, but structural considerations such as the need for a hard-wearing species for moving or rubbing parts should always be borne in mind.

**The carcase**—The bulk of this piece consists of two nearly equal boxes, the upper one fitted with drawers and the lower one constituting a cupboard. The top, bottom, and sides of the boxes are formed by what began as two lengths of walnut, edge-jointed to provide the requisite width, which were then cut to form the four pieces needed for each box (*Figure 83*).

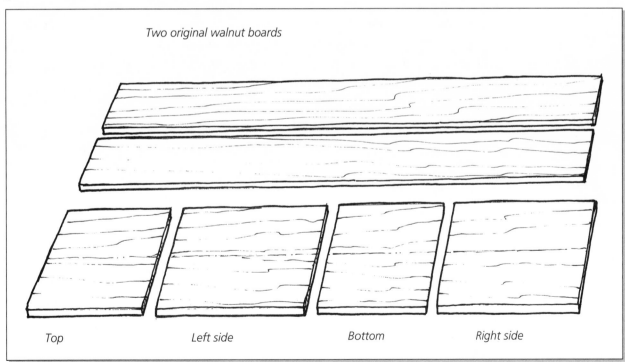

Two original walnut boards

Top     Left side     Bottom     Right side

Although it is more convenient if you can start with boards that are long enough to form all four sides, shorter pieces can be used. Wider boards will necessitate less work, but in any event remember to match the sides of the upper box with the sides of the lower box because both will be visible in the finished piece, and strongly mismatched grain patterns will produce a discordant effect.

*Figure 83
Preparation of one case's sides*

Because all four sides are made with the grain running in the same direction, there will be no problem with uneven wood movement. The front will be totally unaffected since it consists of drawers and doors not fixed to the sides, but the back poses a different problem. Cheap cabinets are typically provided with a plywood back nailed directly on the back or perhaps set in a rabbet. A solid back is a different matter; whichever way it is oriented, it will always be in conflict with the case to which it is fixed in one direction.

Frame-and-panel construction solves this difficulty. The panels, which comprise the largest area of the back, are free to move within the frames as the humidity changes and the wood swells or contracts. The frames, being of much smaller dimensions, constitute little threat to the structural integrity because any change in their width is relatively minor.

It is possible to fix the paneled back directly to the back edges of the carcase, but by setting it in a small rabbet the sides remain unspoiled by the possibility of ill-matched sidegrain of the edges of the backs. Furthermore, setting the frame within the sides provides a stronger method of ensuring that the structure will be square.

You don't need to do anything to accommodate the drawers or cupboard door at this stage, but before starting work on the dovetails that join the two boxes; cut the rabbet for the paneled back. This will prevent the mistake of laying out the dovetails awkwardly. The rabbet can be cut on the tablesaw, the jointer, with a router, or by hand using a rabbet plane. Whichever method you choose, mark all four pieces of each box carefully before you start to avoid any confusion regarding front and back and inside and outside. The rabbet should be formed on the back inside corner of all four pieces. The width of the rabbet must equal the thickness of the proposed framing of the back so that it will sit flush with the back edges of the sides. The depth of the rabbet need be no more than one-third the thickness of the sides (*Figure 84*).

*Figure 84
Proportions of
rabbet*

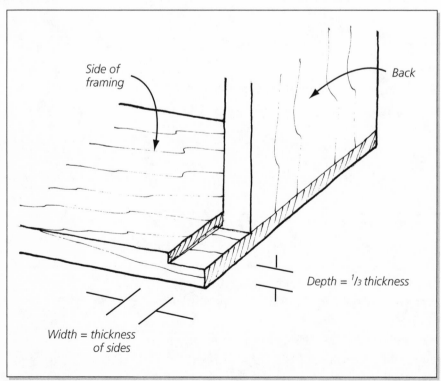

Side of
framing

Back

Depth = ¹/₃ thickness

Width = thickness
of sides

**Special dovetails**—After all pieces have been cut perfectly square and to the proper width and length and appropriately rabbeted, lay out the dovetails so that the square ends of the tails are visible at the sides. This provides the sides with the maximum resistance to being pulled apart.

At the front edge of the case the dovetailing is mitered. This presents a better appearance than the butted edges that would otherwise result. The rabbet at the rear edge also requires special treatment. If a normal dovetail were formed here, the rabbet would result in a gap. You can avoid this by setting the dovetail farther in from the edge than usual and then making a square cut on the tail, level with the rabbet, and then cutting the tail short, or by making the square cut on the tail as before but leaving it full length, removing a corresponding amount level with the rabbet from the pin (*Figure 85*).

Cut the mitered dovetail at the front similarly to the rabbeted dovetail: The end tail is cut with a square side and its whole end is mitered. When you cut the corresponding miter in the pin, take care not to cut the miter deeper than the width of the tail, or a gap will result around the first pin. *Figure 86* makes this joint clear. The most important thing to remember is to cut on the waste side of the miter line, otherwise the joint will not be tight. It is better to leave a little too much, assemble the joint, and then saw through the resultant bulging miter with your thinnest dovetail saw. The wood removed by the kerf should be sufficient to allow the joint to close tightly, because both sides of the miter will have been made by the same cut.

**Frame-and-paneling**—The backs of the two boxes and the cupboard door are made to a similar pattern, their respective overall sizes being measured directly from the assembled cases. Don't glue the cases together when taking these measurements since the finished backs will make this job easier by keeping the cases square.

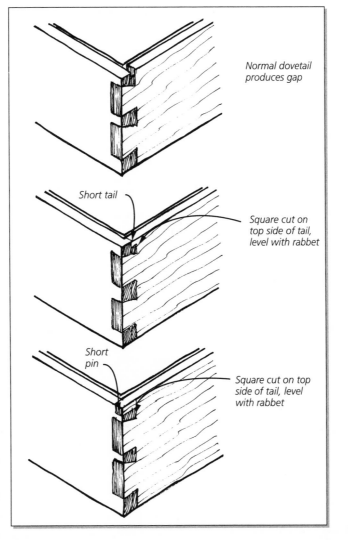

Normal dovetail produces gap

Short tail

Square cut on top side of tail, level with rabbet

Short pin

Square cut on top side of tail, level with rabbet

Figure 85
Dovetailing rabbet

Figure 86  Mitered dovetail

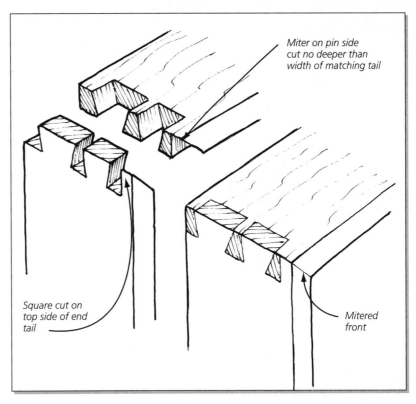

Miter on pin side cut no deeper than width of matching tail

Square cut on top side of end tail

Mitered front

Cut the frame members to length and width and mark each piece to show its relative position. Cut a groove equal to the thickness and plane of the proposed tenons on all members on their inside edges. Whether you use the tablesaw, router, or plough plane to form the grooves, make sure they are all in the same plane by laying them out always from their face side. For maximum strength, plan on centered tenons about one-third the thickness of the framing.

Whether you cut the mortises or the tenons first is up to you, but all joints should be made and tested for fit and flatness of the whole framing before preparing the panels. Although the grooves for the panels are cut in the center of the framing, the matching tongues on the panels can be cut so that the panels fit flush with, recessed in, or proud to the framing. *Figure 87* shows two methods of preparing the panels' edges.

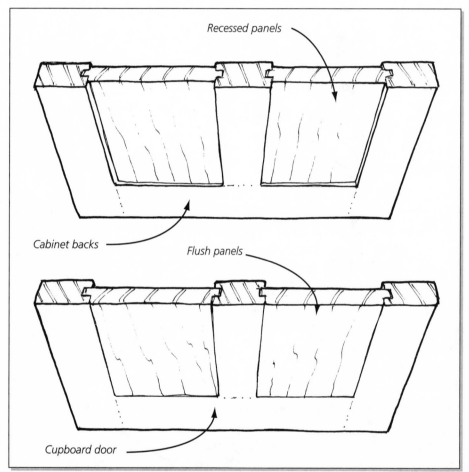

*Figure 87  Recessed
and flush panels*

After you glue up the frames—taking care not to allow any glue into the panel grooves, as the panels must be free to float—finish-plane the two backs and use them to keep the carcase square when this is glued and assembled. The cupboard door should be ⅛ inch smaller all round than is its opening, and its opening edge should be beveled about 15° to allow it to open and close easily, but you need not hang it until both cases are fixed together and the interior is complete.

**Drawer**—The drawers fit flush with the front of the upper case. Since there is thus no overhang or lipping to hide any gaps, you must measure the drawer fronts *very* exactly, allowing no more than a ¹⁄₁₆-inch gap all round.

As well as preparing the stock carefully to fit, pay attention to the effects created by arranging the drawer fronts in different orders. Not only should the color and grain of adjacent drawers look well together, but their relative sizes should be considered as well. If you place the largest at the bottom, a comfortable feeling of balance will be obtained. The rate at which each superior drawer diminishes in height is also important.

After you prepare the fronts and mark them to show front, top, and relative order, make the sides. These need not be as thick as the fronts, which have to accommodate lapped dovetails, but should still be thick enough to accommodate the ¼-inch-deep groove for the runners on which they will ride (*Figure 88*). The drawer backs may be even thinner, although it is easier to cut the through dovetails that will join them to the sides if both pieces are the same thickness. Cut the sides the same height as the fronts and short enough to allow the drawer front to be pushed in flush with the sides. For safety's sake, leave a little extra room here since the alignment of the fronts is managed by careful positioning of the runners in the grooves.

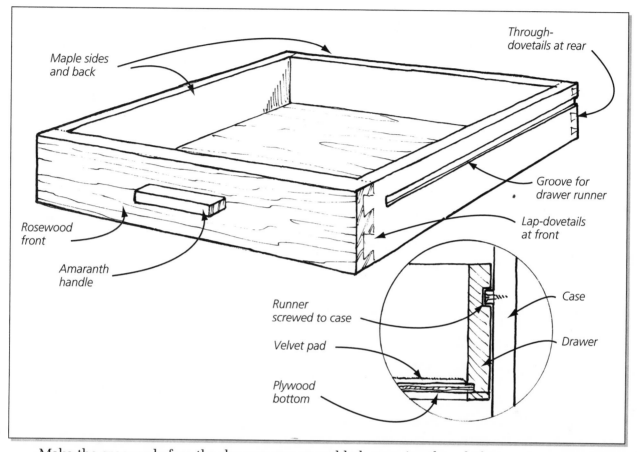

Maple sides and back

Through-dovetails at rear

Groove for drawer runner

Lap-dovetails at front

Rosewood front

Amaranth handle

Runner screwed to case

Velvet pad

Plywood bottom

Case

Drawer

*Figure 88 Drawer details*

Make the grooves before the drawers are assembled, stopping them before they reach the front of the drawer but allowing them to run all the way out at the back. Lay out the through-dovetails for the sides and back so that the groove does not hit a tail. Take similar precautions when laying out the lap-dovetails at the front, but note that here the groove for the drawer bottom *should* run through a tail so that its end will be covered by the drawer front.

Although the top of the back is level with the top of the sides and the front, it is only as deep as the top of the groove cut in the sides for the drawer bottom.

Cut the bottoms from ¼-inch plywood, to which there should be no objection because the interior of the drawers will be lined and plywood is more stable than a thin sheet of solid wood. If the bottoms are cut exactly square, they will help keep the drawer square when it is glued and assembled.

Attach the handles to the completed drawers, first locating the screw holes which hold them from the inside, with all drawers stacked in the order they will occupy in the case. By subtly decreasing the size of the handles proportionately to the decreasing height of the drawers, and by fixing the larger ones slightly closer to the tops of the drawers than those of the smaller drawers, whose handles are more nearly centered, you will produce an effect more elegant than the arbitrary centering of each handle on its drawer.

Prepare runners for the drawers from very smooth and straight strips of maple that fit snugly in the grooves cut in the drawer sides. Slot-screw the runners to the sides of the carcase so that they can be adjusted to allow each drawer to close perfectly flush with the front of the cabinet and will accommodate any movement of the carcase (*Figure 89*). Install the runners from the bottom up, using a piece of thin card as spacer between drawers.

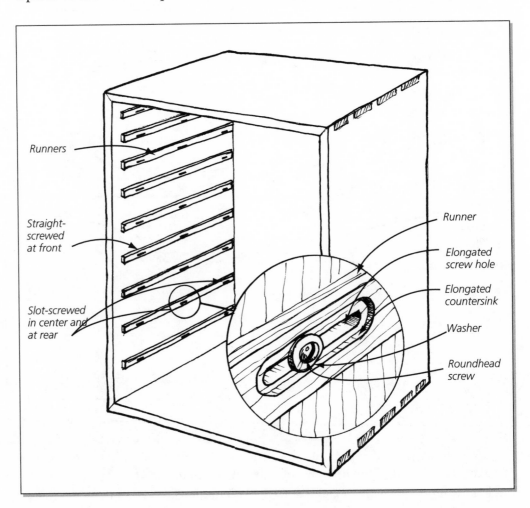

Runners

Straight-
screwed
at front

Slot-screwed
in center and
at rear

Runner

Elongated
screw hole

Elongated
countersink

Washer

Roundhead
screw

*Figure 89 Slot-
screwed drawer
runners*

**The cupboard**—The lower case contains an adjustable shelf made from a walnut board fitted with cleats in the breadboard fashion to keep it flat. There are several ways to do this: The board may have tongues formed on its ends over which the grooved cleat is fitted, fixed only at its center; the board itself may be grooved and the cleat formed with a matching tongue; or both board and cleat may be grooved and held together with a separate spline. Particularly elegant is a long, sliding dovetail cut in the cleat, although a simple square-tongued cleat is stronger.

To be adjustable, the shelf is supported on removable shelf supports that may be arranged in a series of holes bored directly in the inside of the case. Use a boring template to bore all four columns of holes; this will guarantee that all the holes are aligned. Their spacing is a matter of the degree of adjustability you need. To avoid boring completely through the case walls, use a depth stop on the drill bit.

Hang the door so that its front is flush with the front of the case. For a neat appearance, use knife hinges at top and bottom. If regular cabinet butts are used, position them so that they relate equally to the top and bottom rails of the door frame, setting the bottom hinge farther from the bottom than the top hinge is set from the top. This is a small detail, but one that adds to the subtlety of the design.

The door handle is similar to the drawer handles, fixed from within by a countersunk woodscrew. A bullet catch installed in the bottom edge of the door is the neatest way to ensure an aligned closure and additionally provide a measure of anti-sag support to the heavy rosewood frame.

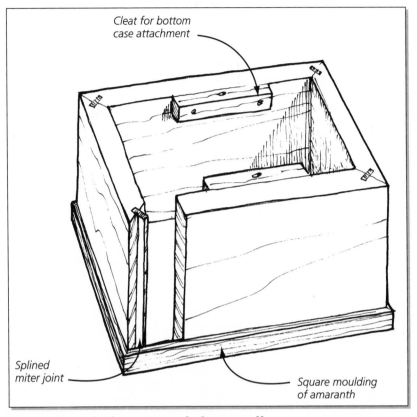

**The base**—The base consists of a simple four-sided box joined with a splined miter joint and finished with a square mini-plinth of mitered amaranth (*Figure 90*). If the stock used to make the sides of the base is thinner than 1 inch, screw a thicker cleat around the inside top edge through which the screws that connect the base to the bottom case can be inserted.

**The top**—Make the top in two parts: a simple cleated cover similar to the cupboard shelf but with mitered ends to the cleats at the front (*Figure 91*), so that no end-grain is visible, and a supporting frame of amaranth that matches the mini-plinth on the base. Bore a hole vertically through the center of each side of the amaranth frame and use this as a template

*Figure 90 Base construction*

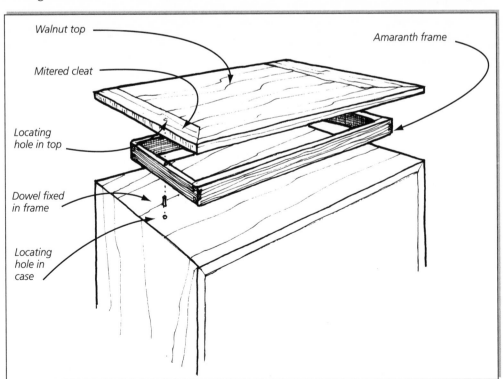

*Figure 91*

to bore matching holes in the top of the upper case and the underneath of the cover. Glue dowels into the frame that project ¼ inch on both sides, just enough to engage the matching holes in cover and case. The top thus forms a shallow secret compartment.

**Assembly**—Screw the base to the bottom case through the cleat provided around the inside of the top of the base, centering the base on the case. Screw the top case to the bottom case by screwing up through the top of the bottom case, taking care to use screws short enough not to protrude into the top case.

**Finishing**—Rosewood and amaranth are such dense woods that little more than a little paste wax was necessary to bring out their rich color. The walnut case may be given a well-rubbed coat or two of oil. The choice of finish is a matter of personal preference and a function of the wood used to construct the piece. While such a piece does not need as protective a finish as would a tabletop, it is still important to treat all surfaces evenly in order to equalize any effect that changing moisture conditions may have, or unequal absorption will set up unequal stresses, with possibly damaging results.

## CUTTING LIST

---

**Top and bottom carcases:**
|   |   |   |
|---|---|---|
| 2 | top sides | .30″ x 15″ x ⅞″ |
| 18 | drawer runners | .12½″ x ¾″ x ¾″ |
| 2 | bottom sides | .21″ x 15″ x ⅞″ |
| 2 | tops | .21″ x 15″ x ⅞″ |
| 2 | bottoms | .21″ x 15″ x ⅞″ |

**Top back panel:**
|   |   |   |
|---|---|---|
| 2 | stiles | .29″ x 2½″ x ¾″ |
| 1 | top rail | .16½″ x 2⅜″ x ¾″ |
| 1 | bottom rail | .16½″ x 3⅞″ x ¾″ |
| 1 | muntin | .24⅜″ x 3″ x ¾″ |
| 2 | panels | .23″ x 6¼″ x ¾″ |

**Bottom back panel:**
|   |   |   |
|---|---|---|
| 2 | stiles | .19⅝″ x 2½″ x ¾″ |
| 1 | top rail | .16½″ x 2⅜″ x ¾″ |
| 1 | bottom rail | .16½″ x 3⅞″ x ¾″ |
| 1 | muntin | .15″ x 3″ x ¾″ |
| 2 | panels | .13½″ x 6¼″ x ¾″ |

**Drawers:**
|   |   |   |
|---|---|---|
| 6 | fronts | .19⅜″ x 2¾″ x ¾″ |
| 6 | backs | .19⅜″ x 2¼″ x ½″ |
| 12 | sides | .13½″ x 2¾″ x ½″ |
| 2 | fronts | .19⅜″ x 3⅜″ x ¾″ |
| 2 | backs | .19⅜″ x 2⅞″ x ½″ |
| 4 | sides | .13½″ x 3⅜″ x ½″ |
| 1 | front | .19⅜″ x 4⅝″ x ¾″ |

1  back . . . . . . . . . . . . . . . . . . . . . . . . . .19⅜″ x 4″ x ½″

2  sides . . . . . . . . . . . . . . . . . . . . . . . . .13½″ x 4⅝″ x ½″

9  bottoms . . . . . . . . . . . . . . . . . . . . . . .13¼″ x 18½″ x ¼″

(luan plywood)

10  handles (dor drawers and door) . . . . . . . . .4″ x 1″ x ½″

**Door:**

2  stiles . . . . . . . . . . . . . . . . . . . . . . . . . . .19½″ x 3⅜″ x ¾″

1  top rail . . . . . . . . . . . . . . . . . . . . . . . . .14½″ x 3⅜″ x ¾″

1  bottom rail . . . . . . . . . . . . . . . . . . . . . .14½″ x 4″ x ¾″

1  muntin . . . . . . . . . . . . . . . . . . . . . . . . .13″ x 3″ x ¾″

2  panels . . . . . . . . . . . . . . . . . . . . . . . . .12½″ x 5″ x ¾″

1  shelf (inclusive of cleats) . . . . . . . . . . . . . .19″ x 12″ x ¾″

**Base:**

1  front . . . . . . . . . . . . . . . . . . . . . . . . . . .16″ x 12″ x ¾″

1  back . . . . . . . . . . . . . . . . . . . . . . . . . . .16″ x 12″ x ¾″

2  sides . . . . . . . . . . . . . . . . . . . . . . . . . .11″ x 12″ x ¾″

2  long plinth pieces . . . . . . . . . . . . . . . . .16½″ x 2″ x ½″

2  short plinth pieces . . . . . . . . . . . . . . . . .12½″ x 2″ x ½″

2  screwing cleats . . . . . . . . . . . . . . . . . .6″ x ¾″ x ¾″

**Top:**

2  short pieces . . . . . . . . . . . . . . . . . . . . .13″ x 2″ x ½″

2  long pieces . . . . . . . . . . . . . . . . . . . . . .19″ x 2″ x ½″

Top (inclusive of cleats) . . . . . . . . . . . . . . . . .15″ x 12″ x ¾″

2  pins . . . . . . . . . . . . . . . . . . . . . . . . . . .2½″ x ¼-inch diameter

**Hardware:**

1  pair 2-inch cabinet butts

1  bullet catch

4  shelf supports

54  #8 x 1-½-inch roundhead woodscrews

54  ⅜-inch flat washers

1  dozen #8 x 1-¼-inch flathead woodscrews

# Glazed credenza

*New uses for old furniture types*

When faced with the task of designing a piece of furniture to fulfill a specific function, you can either start completely from scratch; evolving your own form to suit the occasion, or, as is more usually the case, look to existing examples of the class of object needed to see how others have solved the problem. A third way is to adapt pieces originally developed for purposes other than yours. The glazed credenza described in this chapter was designed to house unusual and oversized books with more safety than is offered by the usual open system of bookcases while still being able to display them to better advantage than would be possible if they were simply hidden away in a locked cabinet. It was also important to provide a place where the books could be opened and examined without having to be taken to a separate table or other piece of furniture.

Other designs might have been used with equal success. Indeed, even a cursory inspection of "bookcases" as a type of furniture will quickly reveal a class of furniture distinctly schizophrenic in character in comparison to more monolithic groups such as tables and chairs which, despite an almost infinite variety of styles, all clearly owe primary allegiance to their avowed functions of providing seating and surface. Bookcases sprang into being long after other types of furniture had been established. It was therefore most natural that they should be derived types rather than *sui generis*. Faced with the necessity of providing for an accumulation of bound books, the first bookcase-makers had a wide variety of existing types of other pieces of furniture to act as their inspiration. As a result, the only form of bookcase that might be considered purely and simply a bookcase is perhaps the simple semi-enclosed system of two or three open shelves, freestanding and usually backed. For the rest, their development may be easily traced to pieces as diverse as medieval hutches, buffets, sideboards, armoires, and even (in the case of so-called lawyer's bookcases) shop-display cabinets.

Contemporary bookcases seem more than many other types of furniture to follow this trend: sloping bookcases designed to lean against a wall are obvious adaptations of the ladder; diagonal bookcases have much in common with wine cellar storage; hanging bookcases are another development. But the cross-fertilization of furniture types which has produced such a variety of bookcases is a useful design principle to bear in mind no matter what piece you are considering. It results most often from combining needs. You require somewhere to sit *and* somewhere to store things and you might end up with the Gothic chair of chapter 14 (or, more likely, a contemporary version). A tall-case clock could be redesigned to house a compact-disc player and a collection of compact discs. The bed that is built over a low system of drawers is another example. The possibilities are endless. The point is not to limit your potential design only to furniture types of the class you want to build.

**The original credenza**—A credenza is not primarily a bookcase. Credenzas come in a variety of shapes and sizes. The term is loosely used to describe things from sideboards to buffets, large chests, low tables, and all sorts of other cabinets. The only characteristic in common among such diverse pieces is a height greater than a table but lower than that of a standing cabinet such as a lowboy or a highboy. The word is Italian and derives from the Latin *credentia,* meaning "security given" or "credentials." It was originally used to describe the practice of putting a nobleman's food and drink on a sideboard or buffet to be tasted by a servant in order to make sure it had not been poisoned before being given to his master. Such sideboards became known in Renaissance Italy as credenzas. The term was gradually extended to cover all sorts of buffets, communion tables, and other pieces of furniture used for fancy china and silverware; in short, any work surface used for something special or valuable. Equally part of the definition is that, in keeping with the style of the Italian Renaissance, credenzas have no legs, but rest directly on the floor.

The glazed credenza is essentially a waist-high cabinet measuring 7 feet long by 20 inches deep. A cabinet is by definition an enclosed construction usually accessed by doors, drop fronts, or lids. In this instance, a series of four glazed doors extend across the entire front, providing complete visibility of the interior while protecting the contents.

The exact measurements are shown in *Figure 92,* but there is no reason why they may not be altered to accommodate other situations, so long as they remain

*Figure 92
Credenza dimensions*

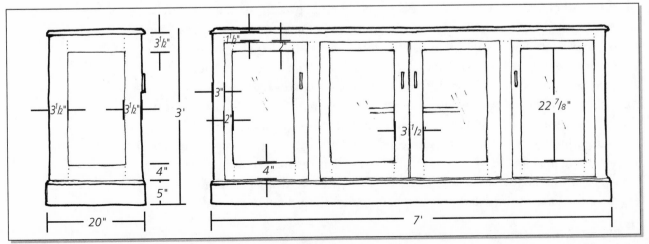

within the broad definition of credenza. It is the overall proportions that are most important. So long as individual members such as rails and stiles are appropriate for the job they have to do, the most important consideration is whether they look well together.

**Materials**—This credenza is built of African mahogany. There are several species commonly available known as mahogany, not all of them true *Swietenias*. African mahogany actually belongs to the genus *Khaya,* related to but separate from the *Swietenias* of various South American countries. It is generally cheaper and more plentiful, and is commonly regarded as inferior to the "real" thing. In fact, although *Swietenias* were originally prized for their greater stability and more interesting figure, much mahogany from Honduras is now very plain, and the Cuban kind is largely unavailable. The plainness of Honduran mahogany is a result of its straight grain, which can be a useful characteristic. African mahogany, on the other hand, is frequently rowed; alternating bands of grain make it hard to machine and work with anything other than the sharpest of handtools. The visual effect, however, of rowed grain is very dramatic, and gives the wood a changing reflective finish of great apparent depth.

Mahogany is an ideal species to carve, being neither excessively hard nor soft. It is not as expensive as other exotics and the relative instability which manifests itself in greater changes in dimension according to the humidity is easily accommodated by frame-and-panel construction.

**Carcase construction**—The carcase consists of a paneled back, sides, and a front frame in which the doors are held. The solid bottom is tongued into the inside of

101
............

**Glazed
credenza**

*Figure 93 Carcase construction*

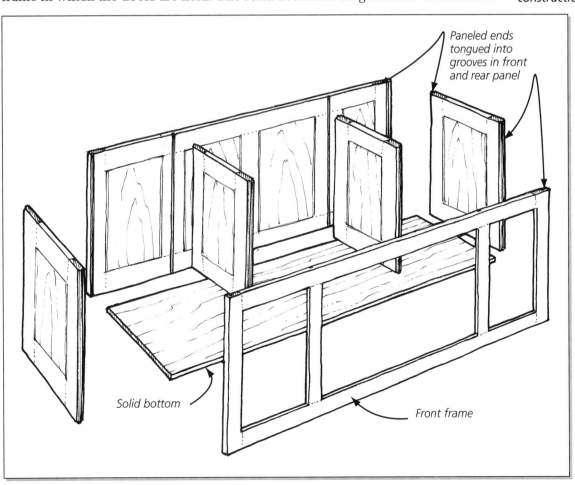

Paneled ends tongued into grooves in front and rear panel

Solid bottom

Front frame

these pieces, and two interior vertical partitions which divide the cabinets into three compartments and provide extra support are similarly grooved into the stiles of the front and back frames (*Figure 93*).

Make the back first. Note that the top and bottom rails are tenoned into the outside stiles, which need not be quite 3 feet high since not only will the top add another ¾ inch to the overall height, but the plinth will add another 1 inch or so at the bottom. The three inside stiles are tenoned into the top and bottom rails, and so are shorter than the outside stiles.

The exact width of all these members will be a function of the size of the panels. While 3 inches is a good width for the top rail and inside stiles, and 4 inches is a good width for the bottom rail and the outside stiles (since these dimensions will produce a frame with nicely proportioned members that are big enough for all the panel grooving), you must feel free to adjust them to accommodate the panels you may make. These will undoubtedly be made up from two or more widths joined together. If you join the available material so that the grain pattern of adjacent parts looks as good as possible, it is all but inevitable that your panels will be other than the specified width. Adjust the framing members accordingly. If you remain insensitive to the individual characteristics of the material you are working with and cut to a predetermined measurement, the finished piece will lack a certain wholeness and be little better than something you could have bought from a factory.

With this in mind, decide on the material you will use to make the panels before starting on the framing. Unless you are certain that the piece will spend its entire life—which could stretch for hundreds of years if you make it right—with its back to the wall, take *both* sides of the panels into account. The glass doors will allow the insides to be equally visible.

Construct the frame (*Figure 94*) as follows: First saw out the stiles and rails to the correct thickness (a minimum of ¾ inch is acceptable, but 1 inch will make the glazing easier). Cut them to the correct widths and lengths, allowing a little

*Figure 94 Rear
frame construction*

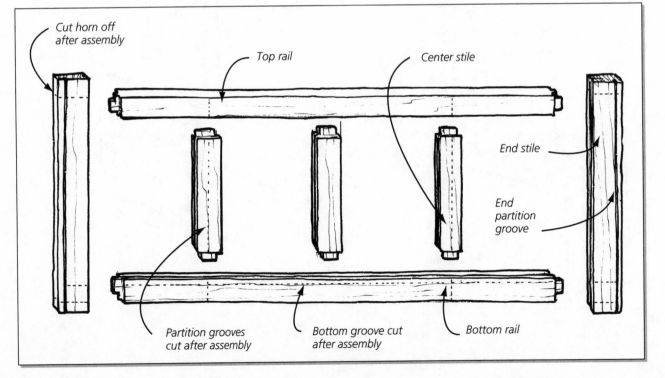

extra length for the outside stiles for purposes of mortising. Groove the inside edges of all members to receive the edges of the panels. Note that the inside stiles must be grooved on both edges. If the rails and stiles are ¾ inch thick, cut a centered groove about ¼ inch wide. Whether you do this by hand using a plough plane or a multiplane, or by machine using a router, shaper, or tablesaw, it is easiest to run the groove the entire length of the member.

Next, cut the tenons on the ends of the rails of the central stiles to the same thickness and in the same plane as the grooves. The tenons at the ends of the rails must be haunched to fill the outside ends of the grooves in the outside stiles. Use the finished tenons to locate their mortises precisely.

It will be most efficient to repeat this process now for both ends before directing your attention to the panels. Apart from the fact that the end frames contain only a single panel each, there is one other important difference between them and the back frame. This concerns the tongues that are formed on the outside edges of the ends' stiles. These tongues fit into corresponding grooves cut in the front and back frames, thereby joining all four sides securely and in correct alignment (*Figure 95*). Do not forget to allow for these tongues when cutting the

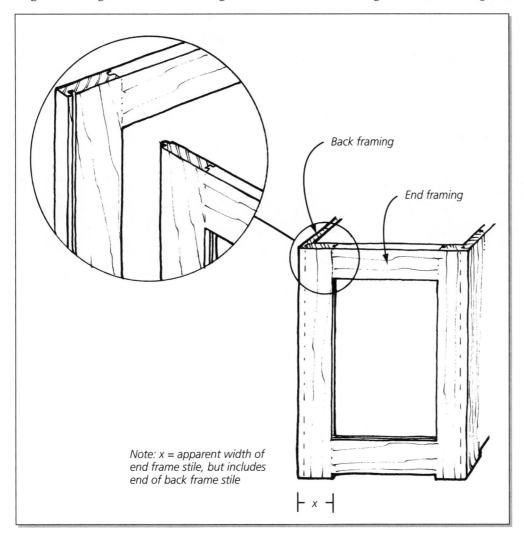

Back framing

End framing

Note: *x* = apparent width of end frame stile, but includes end of back frame stile

├ *x* ┤

*Figure 95  Carcase grooving*

stiles for the ends. Furthermore, the thickness of the front and back frames must similarly be taken into account when deciding on the width of the ends' stiles. To achieve an *apparent* end stile width of 4 inches, for example, the actual stile will measure 4 inches less than the thickness of the front or back stile to which it is joined—plus whatever is needed to form the tongue.

**The panels**—Unless you have unusually wide stock, you will have to join boards to produce sufficiently wide panels. This may be extra work but it does have its advantages. First, you can have fun arranging the constituent parts of each panel-to-be so that the combined grain patterns are more meaningful and effective. Second, you will lessen the amount of contraction and expansion that might occur with a wide single board.

Do not overlook this last point. Depending on the species of wood, its condition when used, and its final location, it will change dimension no matter how long it or the piece of furniture it forms part of has been around. One purpose of frame-and-panel construction is to accommodate such change. It is therefore important to leave enough room for expansion of the panel in the grooves and to provide tongues long enough to continue to fit in the grooves should the panel shrink. A 20-inch-wide panel of African mahogany, even if made of material supposedly air-dried (usually more stable than kiln-dried material), can contract and expand by as much as ½ inch. Unless you have allowed for such movement the panels could either fall out of the framing or expand so much that they burst it.

The panels are the same thickness as the framing. Their tongues are centered, as are the grooves that contain them. They are thus flush with the framing. There is little movement to be expected along the grain, so the top and bottom of each panel may be cut square to ride virtually flush against the rails. The sides, however, are beaded (*Figure 96*) to disguise any expansion or contraction across the grain.

*Figure 96 Panel details*

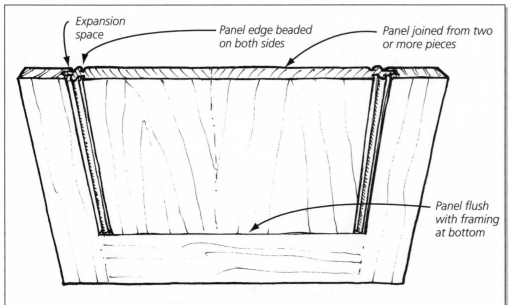

**The front frame**—The frame in which the doors are hung is made similarly to the back frame but without any panel grooves. The end stiles do need grooves, however, to receive the end stiles' tongues. The dimensions of the rails and stiles are somewhat narrower than those of the back because the door frames have to be taken into account in order to match the proportion of the rest of the framing. Furthermore, you must align the two central stiles with the central stiles of the back so that the partitions will fit properly.

**Partitions and floor**—Having made and assembled the front, side, and back framing, you must groove them for the partitions, floor, and buttons before joining them together. The reason for grooving after assembly of these parts is that the grooves necessarily run through both rails and stiles.

The partitions, which may be either solid or frame-and-panel, fit into vertical grooves cut in the back of the front frame's stiles and the front of the back frame's stiles. You may make them as thick as the partition but the extra work involved in making tongues as shown in *Figure 97* will avoid the necessity of worrying about how well the joint fits, since the shoulders either side of the tongue will hide any small inconsistencies and make assembly easier.

The floor (*Figure 98*) is similarly tongued and fitted into matching grooves cut in the back and sides only. At the front, the floor projects ¼ inch above the top of the front frame's bottom rail in order to provide a stop for the doors, so there is no tongue and groove here. Three or four 1–inch by 1–inch blocks are sufficient to secure the front of the floor from below to the front frame, leaving the rest of the floor—which is solid and consequently subject to contraction and expansion—free to float in the grooves at the side and back. For this purpose, make the tongue on the floor flush with its top surface rather than being centered as on the partition. In this way any contraction will be invisible and no gap will form into which small items might fall.

The last groove to be made is the one to receive the buttons that will secure the

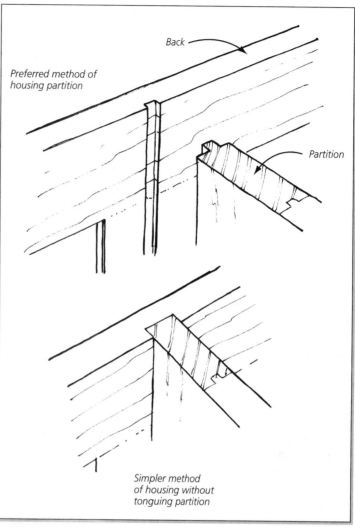

Preferred method of housing partition

Back

Partition

Simpler method of housing without tonguing partition

*Figure 97 Partition housing*

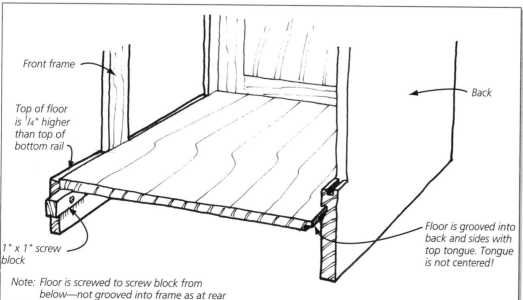

Front frame

Top of floor is ¼" higher than top of bottom rail

1" x 1" screw block

Note: Floor is screwed to screw block from below—not grooved into frame as at rear

Back

Floor is grooved into back and sides with top tongue. Tongue is not centered!

*Figure 98 Floor details*

top of the credenza to the framing. This groove is cut near the top inside face of all four frames according to the buttons or tabletop fasteners you intend to use.

Final assembly, while a considerable undertaking, is largely self-regulating so far as alignment and squareness are concerned as a result of the way the constituent parts are grooved and fit together. The order is: sides and partitions into the back; floor; then front.

**The plinth**—The plinth is extremely simple, consisting of four lengths of 5-inch-wide skirting, moulded along its top edge, and carefully mitered at all four corners. Its thickness will depend on the profile of the moulding you choose for its top edge—or vice-versa! Fix it by screwing through from the inside of the framing, leaving a ¼-inch reveal between its top and the top of the front frame's bottom rail (*Figure 99*).

*Figure 99  Plinth details*

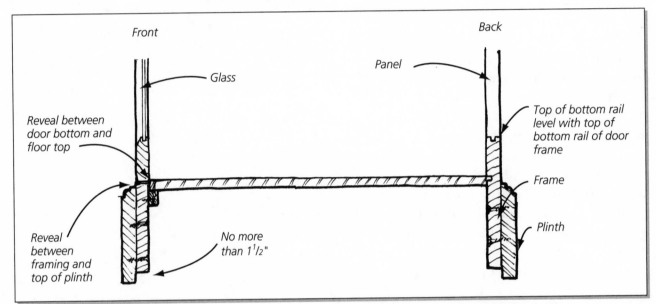

The top—Choose the very best boards available for the top because this will be as visible as a tabletop. Allow a sufficient overhang all around, taking into account that the front and back are bound to move a little with changing moisture conditions. The edge may be moulded and even carved as in the photograph. If you use rowed African mahogany, make sure to use well-sharpened scrapers to finish the surface since sanding will achieve a smooth surface but will destroy the wonderful changing reflective quality this wood has by abrading the ends of the fibers instead of cutting them off cleanly.

It is best to bore the holes for the adjustable shelf supports before screwing down the top. Use a template as a boring guide to ensure that the holes are all aligned, and use a depth stop to avoid inadvertently boring completely through any member. The shelves should be cleated to keep them flat, as described in chapter 11. Unlike the mitered cleats used for the top of the standing cabinet, the cleats may run from front to back on each shelf since their front ends will be hidden behind the front framing. Fix the top to the framing with buttons. These should be especially firmly fixed in the middle of its ends, so that those at the front and back are able to slide in their grooves as the top shrinks and expands.

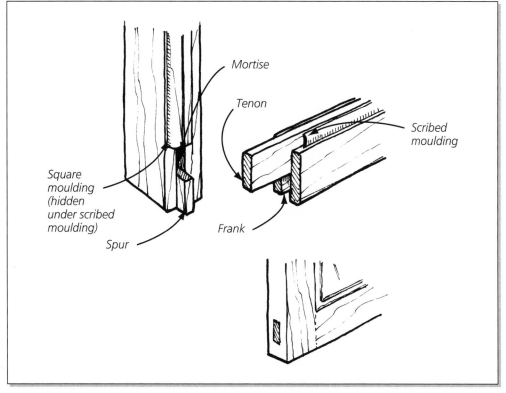

Mortise

Tenon

Scribed
moulding

Square
moulding
(hidden
under scribed
moulding)

Frank

Spur

*Figure 100  Glazed
door frame details*

**The glazed doors**—With sufficient foresight and prudence, any change of dimensions will have still ensured that the rails and stiles of each door are substantial enough to receive the moulding and rabbet for the glass, hinges, and—in the case of the two central doors—the meeting rabbets. It is important, too, that they continue to match the proportions of the adjacent framing of the ends of the credenza.

The door frames are constructed similarly to the other framing but without the groove necessary for the panels. Instead, you must form a rabbet for the glass on the inside edges. The outer edge is moulded, and in order that this part may meet in a miter at the corners, the mortise and tenons must be cut as shown at *Figure 100*. This form of joint, common to glazed framing, has a frank to receive the central part of the moulding rather than a haunch to fit in the panel groove. You can, of course, construct the joint without the frank but you will lose the advantages that it offers in terms of keeping the framing in the same plane. In the case of this credenza, this is especially important since there are no mullions, muntins, or extra sash bars to help keep the frame out of winding.

The thickness of the tenon should equal the central part of the moulding. The rabbet should be wide enough to accommodate the glass and the ¼-inch quarter-round restraining moulding. If you have used the tablesaw to make the various tongues or rabbets you will have produced enough square-sectioned waste that can be used to make these strips. Fix the strips with small roundhead brass pins; these are easy to remove should the glass ever need replacing. Make them a little over-length so that they must be sprung gently into place. This will help keep them tight and ensure that the glass does not rattle in its frame.

Bead the outside edges of the stiles to continue the design of the paneling and help disguise any unevenness in the gap between door and frame. The bead ideally should be the same diameter as the hinge knuckle.

The meeting stiles of the center doors are mutually rabbeted (*Figure 101*). Take care that from the front they meet in the center of the bead cut in the right-hand door; this requires that the right-hand stile be made that much wider than the left-hand stile.

Attach the handles with screws inserted from behind the frame and then hang the doors. Each door should close against the ¼-inch reveal formed by the floor of the credenza and the plinth. You can further guarantee perfect closing by making the front of the shelving flush with the back of the door frame. Use magnetic catches in the area behind the handles or install bullet catches at the base of the opening stiles to keep the doors properly closed.

**Finishing**—How you finish is a matter of personal choice and depends on the species used. This piece is an excellent candidate for a sprayed lacquer finish, but several coats of danish oil will also work very nicely. The top needs perhaps a little more protection than does the rest of the piece and should be treated as a tabletop.

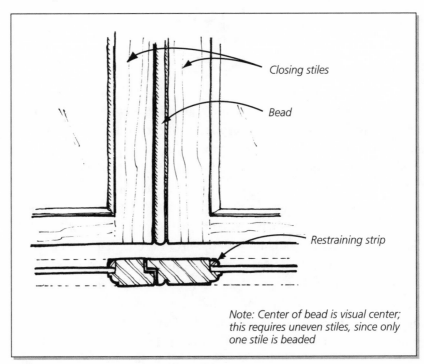

*Figure 101  Meeting
stiles detail*

Closing stiles

Bead

Restraining strip

Note: Center of bead is visual center; this requires uneven stiles, since only one stile is beaded

1 top . . . . . . . . . . . . . . . . . . . . .84″ x 20″ x ¾″

*(The following is provided as a convenient checklist of parts needed. See text for remarks concerning dimensions of individual members.)*

**Back frame:**
2 stiles
3 muntins
1 top rail
1 bottom rail
4 panels
Overall width . . . . . . . . . . . . . . . . . . . . . . . . .82½″
Overall height . . . . . . . . . . . . . . . . . . . . . . . . .34″

**Ends:**
4 stiles
2 top rails
2 bottom rails
2 panels
Overall width . . . . . . . . . . . . . . . . . . . . . . . . .18½″
Overall height . . . . . . . . . . . . . . . . . . . . . . . . .34″

**Partitions:**
4 stiles
4 rails
4 panels

**Front frame:**
2 stiles
2 muntins
1 top rail
1 bottom rail
Overall width . . . . . . . . . . . . . . . . . . . . . . . . .82½″
Overall height . . . . . . . . . . . . . . . . . . . . . . . . .34″

**Doors:**
 8 stiles
 4 top rails
 4 bottom rails
16 restraining strips . . . . . . . . . . . . . . . . . . . .length as needed ″ x ¼″ x ¼″
 4 handles . . . . . . . . . . . . . . . . . . . . . . . . .4″ x 1″ x ¾″
 4 shelves (to fit between partitions as needed)
 1 Floor . . . . . . . . . . . . . . . . . . . . . . . . .83¼″ x 19¼″
 4 screw blocks . . . . . . . . . . . . . . . . . . . . . . . . .3″ x 1″ x 1″

**Plinth:**
2 long pieces . . . . . . . . . . . . . . . . . . . . . . . . .84″ x 5″ x ¾″
2 short pieces . . . . . . . . . . . . . . . . . . . . . . . . .20″ x 5″ x ¾″

**Hardware:**

12 tabletop fasteners (and screws) or buttons

4 pairs of 2-inch cabinet butts

4 bullet catches or magnetic catches

½ gross #8 x 1½-inch flathead woodscrews

4 panes of glass for doors

1 box restraining strip brads

# Pepysian bookcase

*Working in previous styles*

Chapter 12 dealt with adjusting existing designs, and specifically designs of other furniture types, to produce a new piece where the purpose and utilitarian function were the main considerations. This chapter suggests mining the past for a different reason, namely style. This may be done regardless of function insofar as the piece in question's style is indeed independent of its function.

Different periods of history have produced different styles of furniture. How the styles relate to the tenor and exigencies of the times is relevant to an understanding of their genesis and to a greater appreciation of their characteristics than might be apparent to an observer ignorant of their place in history. A certain aesthetic, however, is bound to strike a chord in a sensitive observer no matter how far removed in time and place. Some things speak to us across centuries and cultures simply because we respond—sometimes without knowing why—to their shape, their color, their presence, or any of a number of other ineffable qualities. We just like them. This is sufficient reason to attempt to use these aspects in something new we might design.

Designing this way is relatively straightforward if the piece we are considering building is of a type that exists in the chosen style. We have only to discover what constitutes the style and apply the same principles, using original examples as our guide. In the case of much medieval furniture, the underlying design parameters were basic geometric shapes chosen for theosophical reasons such as the perfection of infinity (represented by the circle) and the Holy Trinity (represented by the trefoil, the triangle, and other three-sided figures). In the case of much eighteenth-century furniture, the underlying design was based on interpretations of the various proportions of classical architecture. Other styles are defined by more obvious characteristics such as a particular form of decoration. The study of what underlies any given period of furniture is a fascinating pastime, although it can lead to ludicrous results if not properly grasped. Trying to imitate a particular style without a clear understanding of what it is that truly constitutes that style can produce silly and ugly anachronisms. But this ought not to deter you from incorporating elements that appeal to you. The point here is not to define good taste but to become aware of other sources of inspiration.

The situation becomes a little more difficult if you wish to design a piece in a style that was used in a period when the piece itself had not been invented. Chippendale never made any stereo cabinets because there were as yet no stereo systems. He made plenty of tea trays and pier glasses, however, not to mention more common types of furniture such as tables and chairs. If you can ascertain what it is that makes a Chippendale piece quintessentially Chippendale, then there is no reason you cannot build a Chippendale stereo cabinet. This was the motivation for the design of the Pepysian bookcase. The discussion of the construction process illustrates how certain elements were perceived and adapted.

There is a series of bookcases now housed at Cambridge University made for the English diarist Samuel Pepys in 1666 that I have long admired for their size and handsome proportions. Unfortunately, they are much too large for today's average home, and most of my books live in built-in open shelving. But I recently got my chance to build something along the lines of Pepys' "book presses"—as the paneled cupboards designed with glass doors to hold books were called in the seventeenth century—when I came into simultaneous possession of a 16-foot-long, 4-inch-thick, and 16-inch-wide mahogany board, and a high-ceilinged shop.

Glass-fronted bookcases have long been considered the best way to keep books. The volumes can easily be seen, ordered, and cataloged, and at the same time are protected from dust, damp, light, and wear. This was especially important in the days when most books were leather-bound, expensive, and highly prized. Nowadays, even though many books are cheap paperbacks, it is still a great way to maintain your own library. It can also serve as an elegant place to house and display other treasured accumulations, such as china, curios, or, in my case, an ever-growing collection of moulding planes.

**An evolving design**—My original plan was to build a simple case with adjustable shelving, fit it with glass doors so that the contents could be seen while remaining dust-free, mount the case on a stand, and construct a simple cornice so that the finished piece echoed the general proportions of the seventeenth-century bookcases I so admired. These pieces are frequently characterized by a flat cornice, unlike the often high, scrolled bonnets of much Georgian furniture of the succeeding century. They also tend to have heavier, rather squat bases that give the appearance of a waistline lower than a twentieth-century sensibility feels completely comfortable with.

Pepys's book presses were made of oak, as was most furniture of that period. But I was not attempting to build an authentic reproduction, and in any case I had this magnificent piece of mahogany that I thought would provide enough material for the entire cabinet. I also decided to simplify the stand, which in the original consisted of an extra glass-doored case in its own right, standing on bun feet, by building a straightforward ball-and-claw, cabriole-legged stand. This form was as yet unknown in Pepys's day, but it was the overall shape and relative proportions of the various parts that I intended to imitate.

**Materials, dimensions, and tools**—The way I obtained the necessary parts for this piece, all from the same giant board, is detailed here, but should not deter you from constructing a similar piece using more standard sizes of material. It is also important to realize that I followed no exact proportional system in arriving at finished dimensions. To do so was common practice in the eighteenth century, when craftsmen were seeking to emulate the classical styles which are at the heart of much Georgian furniture, but I relied primarily on my eye to achieve the kind of balance I felt was demonstrated by Pepys' cases. I estimated rather than calculated the relationships among the parts, as well as the overall dimensions of height, width, and depth. It is also true that I allowed the available material to dictate certain fundamental dimensions since I wanted to keep the work to a minimum. You should feel similarly free to adapt the measurements given here to your own purposes. If you can appreciate what it is about the original that is so proportionally appealing, by all means change things according to your circumstances and rely on your own eye to preserve the spirit of the original. Apart from the resawing needed to produce the individual boards from my original plank, which was done on a large resawing bandsaw, the entire cabinet was built using only handtools. Since its purpose was to house my various moulding, rabbeting, and other special-purpose planes, this seemed appropriate, but most operations could have been performed just as easily with powertools, such as tablesaws, shapers, routers, and so on.

**Case construction**—Start by preparing the top and bottom and sides of the case. I merely sawed off a little over 6 feet from my board and resawed this to produce the necessary four pieces. After surfacing I ended up with pieces a full ⅞ inch thick. This provides a little more meat for the dovetailing and other joinery that is needed than the standard ¾-inch-thick boards, but using thinner stuff is also possible.

Finish all four pieces to the same width, and let the top and bottom into the sides with lapped dovetails as shown in *Figure 102*. The bottom back edge of the top and the top back edge of the bottom are rabbeted to receive the back panel, so be sure to start the

**113**

............

**Pepysian bookcase**

Figure 102 Case construction and dimensions

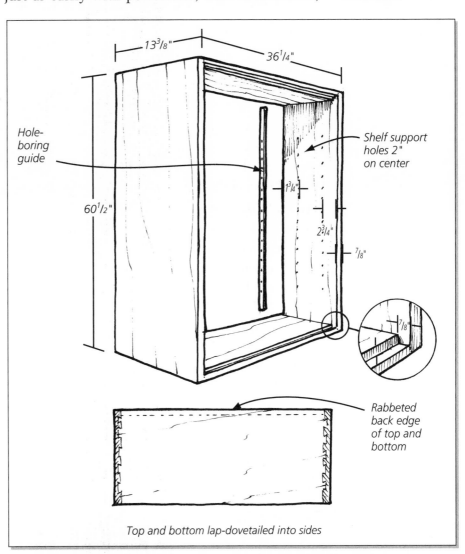

13³/₈"

36¹/₄"

60¹/₂"

Hole-boring guide

1³/₄"

2³/₄"

⁷/₈"

Shelf support holes 2" on center

⁷/₈"

Rabbeted back edge of top and bottom

*Top and bottom lap-dovetailed into sides*

dovetails far enough in from these edges not to interfere with the rabbet. For simplicity's sake, prepare all carcase and frame parts to the same thickness. This resulted in a ⅞-inch-wide rabbet for me; if you are working with ¾-inch stuff, then the rabbet will be ¾ inch wide.

Make the back of the case before gluing the sides to the top and bottom, since the back, if nicely fitted, will help ensure proper squareness when the carcase is in clamps.

The back (*Figure 103*) is simple mortise-and-tenon frame-and-panel construction: two stiles running from top to bottom, joined by three horizontal rails,

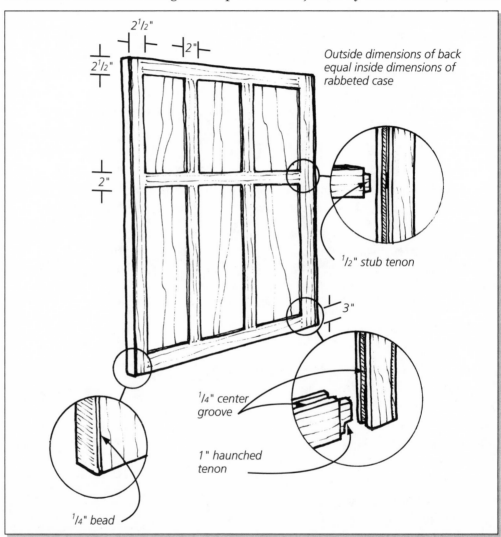

2½"

2½"

2"

2½"

*Outside dimensions of back
equal inside dimensions of
rabbeted case*

2"

*¹/₂" stub tenon*

3"

*¹/₄" center
groove*

*1" haunched
tenon*

*¹/₄" bead*

*Figure 103  Back
construction and
dimensions*

which in turn are separated by two pairs of muntins. The pattern of the framing is largely arbitrary: in my case it was decided by the width of the boards available for resawing into ¼-inch-thick panels. I felt at least one center rail was necessary for strength, but there is no reason why two or more might not be used; it simply entails more joinery.

After preparing all the framing members to length, thickness, and width, cut a ¼-inch-wide and ¼-inch-deep center groove in the inside edges of the stiles, in the top and bottom rails, and in both edges of the muntins and the center rail. Now cut ¼-inch-thick tenons, in the same plane as the groove, at the ends of the rails and muntins. Only the tenons on the top and bottom rails need be very long:

1 inch if the stiles are 1½ inches to 2 inches wide; the tenons on the other members are merely for fixing their location and can be as short as ½ inch.

Lay out the matching mortises directly from the tenons. Note that the tenons at the ends of the top and bottom rails are haunched. It is wise to leave the rails a little longer than their finished size to protect against splitting out the ends of the mortises as they are excavated, and then trim them to length after the frame has been assembled. This is particularly true if you are excavating the mortises by hand with chisel and mallet. It is less important if you are using a plunge router, drill press, or horizontal borer. It is similarly wise to leave the stiles a little wider than necessary so that the assembled back can be trimmed to a perfect fit in the carcase before assembly.

Cut the panels to length and width, leaving a little space all round for any possible expansion should the ambient moisture content increase and the panels become wider. At the same time do not make them so narrow that the slightest shrinking of their width will cause them to pop out of the framing. Getting this right is a matter of considering the species you are using, how well-seasoned it is, how impervious the finish will be, and what the conditions are likely to be where the piece will live.

To minimize the appearance of any possible shrinking, as well as for the sake of neatly recognizing the joint without trying to disguise it, run a ¼-inch bead down the outside back edges of the stiles after the assembled back has been test-fitted in the carcase. When the back has been glued up and trimmed to a perfectly rectangular fit, use it to keep the carcase square while it in turn is glued and clamped, but do not fix it in place.

When the carcase comes out of clamps, remove the back and bore the holes for the shelf supports on the insides of the sides. A strip of one-by-two scrap cut to fit exactly between the top and bottom and bored with a series of ¼-inch holes 2 inches on center makes a perfect boring guide. If the strip is marked and always used the same way up, the two columns of holes necessary on both sides will be in perfect alignment. Now the back can be fixed in place with glue or a screw through the top and bottom rabbet.

**The stand**—Apart from the shaping of the cabriole legs and the carving of the ball-and-claw feet, the construction of the stand is very straightforward, consisting of four legs, four skirts, a simple framed overhang with a submoulding, and a three-sided shoe into which the case fits (*Figure 104*).

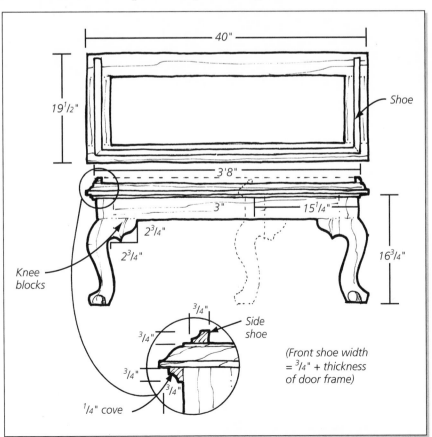

*Figure 104 Stand details*

The legs are prepared from four 16¾-inch lengths of stock that is 4 inches square. If you don't want to attempt cabriole legs, simply prepare four lengths that are 1⅞ inches square. This is the dimension of the square formed at the top of the cabriole leg into which the skirts of the stand are mortised. To cut out the cabriole shape evenly on all legs, use a template made from something thin but stiff, such as hardboard. Leave a 3-inch length at the top that is 1⅞ inches wide. Draw around the template held against two adjacent sides of the leg so that the knee part of the template touches itself (*Figure 105*).

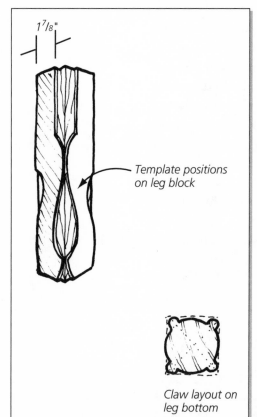

1⁷/₈"

Template positions
on leg block

Claw layout on
leg bottom

*Figure 105  Cabriole
layout*

The usual procedure is to bandsaw to the template lines and then complete the shaping using a drawknife, spokeshaves, rasps, and files. The feet may be carved to a variety of patterns observed either from existing examples or from published patterns. The shapes of the claws and the balls they hold may vary: genuine antiques can often be identified as to their place of manufacture by characteristic shapes common to particular makers or cities such as Philadelphia and New York. The most important point to bear in mind for a well-designed foot is to locate the claws evenly around a circle scribed on the bottom of the foot and then to carve to this line.

Whichever form of leg you choose, excavate the mortises for the tenons of the skirts before you attempt any shaping; the leg is much easier to work on when still square.

I find it preferable to lay out the mortises directly from the tenons at the ends of the skirts. This requires knowing the finished dimension of the square at the top of the leg so that the skirts can be cut to length and then have tenons cut. The skirts are arranged so that their faces are flush with the outsides of the legs. This allows the longest tenons. Their ends should be mitered and almost touch at the bottoms of their respective mortises.

When the joinery is complete—and after any carving has been finished—glue and clamp the legs to the skirts, taking care to preserve the rectilinearity of all four sides. It also helps to perform the assembly on a known flat surface, such as your benchtop, in order to guarantee that the base is not twisted vertically and that all four legs touch the ground at once. If you have made cabriole legs, now is the time to cut out eight 2¾-inch-square knee blocks and glue them to the legs, but not to the underneath of the skirt or they may eventually split should the skirt shrink. The ogee profile is cut before they are glued in position, but the rest of the shaping is left until the glue has dried.

Make a mortise-and-tenoned, or biscuit-joined, frame whose members are 3¾ inches wide. The front and back members should run from end to end so that no endgrain is visible from the front or rear. Whether you use moulding planes or a router to form the ogee profile in the frame's upper outside edge, cut the sides first, using a piece of scrap clamped to the end of the cut. When the profile is formed on the front and back it may be run the entire length with no fear of chipping the ends. Indeed, if any chipping occurred when forming the sides, this will now be removed.

The frame is screwed to the top of the skirts with a single screw in the center of each frame member. Since this is not a solid top there is little danger of sufficient shrinking across the width of the front and back frame members to cause any problems. Make sure that the overhang, which should be about 1 inch all round, is even on all sides.

Prepare a length of moulding, approximately ¾ inch square with a cove formed on one edge, sufficiently long to be cut into four pieces and mitered together against the skirts tight under the overhang. Fix this with small finishing nails, and set and fill the holes.

The shoe for the case is made in three parts. The two side pieces should be about ¾ inch wide so that they can be set in from the upper part of the moulding on the frame's edge by ⅛ inch. Their top outside edge should also be moulded in such a way that the combined profile of shoe, frame, and sub-moulding presents a coherent whole. Without going into details about the usual eighteenth-century reasons for particular profiles and their components—all of which were strictly modeled on classical architecture—suffice it to say that alternating convex with concave shapes and keeping all fillets and arrises (flat edges and corners) in proportion generally produces the most pleasing effect. Before deciding on the exact profile, however, read the next paragraph.

The front piece of the shoe is wider than the side pieces by the thickness of the material you intend to use for the doors to the case. *Figure 106* makes the reason for this clear. It also shows why the height of the shoe must be ¼ inch less than the thickness of the bottom of the case: so that the revealed edge of the case bot-

*Figure 106 Shoe
details*

tom forms a stop for the door. Once you understand the function and limitations of the shoe you will be able to choose an appropriate moulding. Lacking an extensive collection of moulding planes, router bits, or shaper cutters, you can always plane a simple chamfer or bevel along this edge.

The side pieces of the shoe are stop-mitered into the wider front piece. Their rear ends are left square with the back of the case when this is slid into the shoe. All three pieces

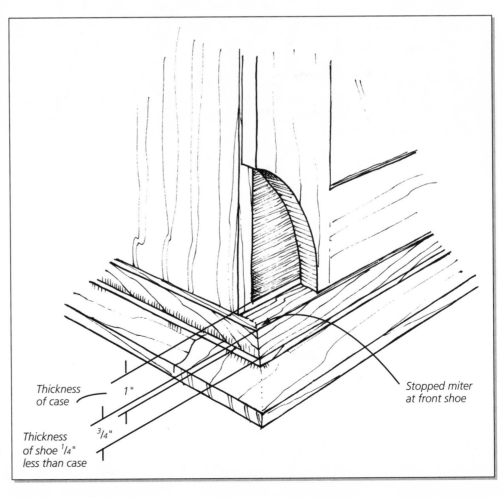

Thickness of case — 1"

Thickness of shoe ¼" less than case — ¾"

Stopped miter at front shoe

of the shoe are screwed to the top of the frame, countersinking and plugging where appropriate.

Apart from the applied carving on the front skirt, which may be greatly simplified or even omitted, the stand is now complete.

**The top**—The basic frame of the top (*Figure 107*) is made to exactly the same width and depth as the case from four lengths 4 inches high. The two side pieces of the frame are blind-dovetailed into the front piece. This joint is sometimes called a secret miter dovetail. Its virtue here is that while a mitered corner joint is preferable in order to avoid any endgrain showing, the dovetailing is an easy way to hold the pieces together without messing around with splines or corner blocks.

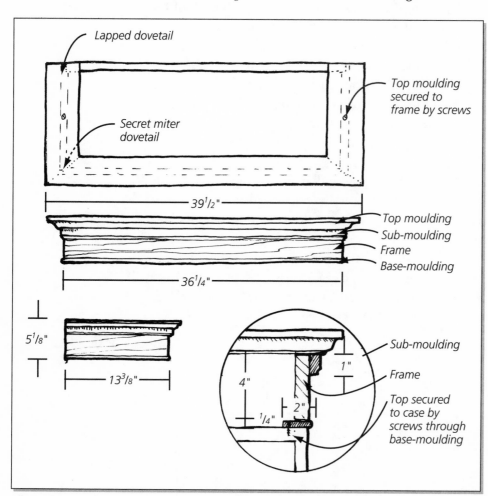

Figure 107

The joint is made by marking the squared ends of both parts of the joint as if for a miter and then making a rabbet that stops at the miter line as shown at *Figure 108* in both ends. Once the rabbet has been formed, the dovetails are cut in that section defined by the rabbet, just as for a double-lapped dovetail, and the remaining square portion left at the ends is trimmed to the miter lines. Do not be afraid to tackle this joint; it is easier than you might think. The secret is to be careful in trimming the ends to the miter lines, and this process can be made almost foolproof if you start carefully with a chisel and trim to the line using a shoulder plane and a very simple guide as shown. If the guide, which can be any piece of scrap as long as the joint is wide, is cut to an accurate 45° and clamped to the end of the joint so that the shoulder plane can run on it, it will be hard to form anything other than a perfect miter. As for the dovetails, since they are invisible and will be sufficiently strong no matter how sloppily they are cut, do not waste time striving for the same degree of perfection as might be justified by visible dovetails.

The back piece is lap-dovetailed into the two side pieces, and then all four pieces may be glued together.

A 2-inch-wide strip of ¼-inch-thick wood, which in my case was conveniently obtained from the offcuts left from the panel material prepared for the case's back, is rounded along its outside edge and glued and screwed to the bottom of the frame sides and front. I formed this round edge with a ¼-inch beading plane. Two passes with a small round-over bit also works. Even a block plane and some sandpaper or a simple scratch stock will accomplish the same thing. Keep the edge even so that only the rounded portion projects past the face of the frame. Note that this strip is not necessary at the back. Its absence creates a gap under the back part of the frame that is useful in earthquake country, where you can secure the cabinet to a wall with a loop of wire passed around the back of the

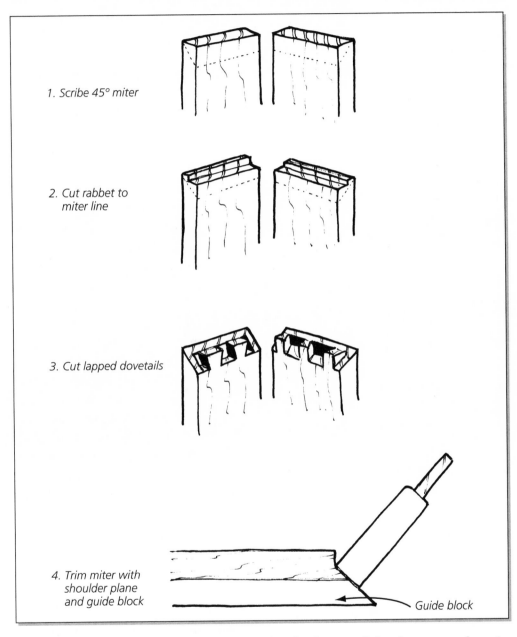

1. Scribe 45° miter

2. Cut rabbet to
   miter line

3. Cut lapped dovetails

4. Trim miter with
   shoulder plane
   and guide block        Guide block

*Figure 108*

frame. The strips are made wider than the thickness of the frame members in order to provide an inside projection through which the top can be screwed to the top of the case.

To the top edge of the front and sides of the frame screw three mitered pieces wide enough to overhang the outside face of the frame by about 1⅝ inches all round. The bottom front edges of these pieces are moulded with the same profile, upside down, as the top outside edges of the frame that was screwed to the top of the stand. In the corner formed by the overhang and the frame, fix a sub-moulding 1 inch high by ½ inch wide, with a ¼-inch cove formed in its bottom outside edge. This piece is similar to the sub-moulding used on the stand. Its extra height seems better proportioned for the top. The rear ends of the moulded pieces fixed to the top of the frame should be trimmed flush with the back of the frame, and any nails used to secure the sub-moulding should be set and filled.

**The doors**—There are several ways to make the doors, depending on what tools you prefer to use. In their simplest form, the doors are a pair of mortise-and-tenoned frames with a small rabbet created on the inside edges to receive a pane of glass which is then secured with a small strip of wood tacked to the frame (*Figure 109*).

*Figure 109 Door
construction*

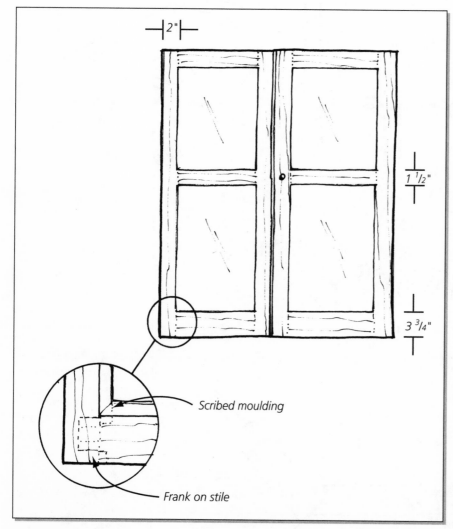

Scribed moulding

Frank on stile

*Figure 110 Meeting
stiles*

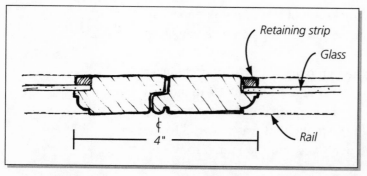

Retaining strip

Glass

Rail

Using ⅞-inch-thick material gave me the opportunity to use a stick and rabbet plane that formed the ovolo moulding on the outside of the frame and the rabbet for the glass on the inside simultaneously. After the rails were tenoned into the stiles, a part of the ovolo moulding was chiseled away and coped to fit the moulded part of the rail. This is better than mitering the two moulded portions because if the rail shrinks across its width, it never reveals a gap.

The meeting edges of the stiles are half-lapped as at *Figure 110*. This allows the first door to be secured to the case when closed with a small barrel or slide bolt at top and bottom, and the second door to be secured to the first door with a simple turn button or mortise lock. The first stile must be wider than the second stile by the width of the lap if both stiles are to appear the same width when closed.

A further adjustment becomes necessary to retain the appearance of symmetry if the edge of the second door is beaded. The advantage of the bead is that its quirk echoes the joint between the doors and makes this less obvious. For best effect, the widths of the stiles should be adjusted so that the distance from the center of the bead, not the quirk or the joint, is the same on both sides. A ¼-inch bead here will add congruity to the piece, since this is the same dimension used elsewhere. Additionally, run a ¼-inch bead down the back outside edges of the doors. Not only will this bead help disguise the gap between door and carcase but the hinge knuckles can be aligned with the bead for a very neat effect.

**The shelving**—How many shelves you need is optional. I wanted as many as possible to house the maximum number of planes. To save valuable mahogany, I edged some used pine with a ½-inch strip of mahogany, and cut a ¼-inch center

bead in the face of the strip (*Figure 111*). Shelving in antique cabinets is frequently made out of a cheaper secondary wood. The aged appearance of the used pine not only looked right but also made sense for the possible abuse it would receive from the cutting edges of my planes.

The last touch was a departure from tradition: Instead of pins or cutout zigzag supports for the shelves, I used brass shelf supports. They are neat, easy to use, and match the brass hinges. I am sure Samuel Pepys would have approved had they been available in 1666.

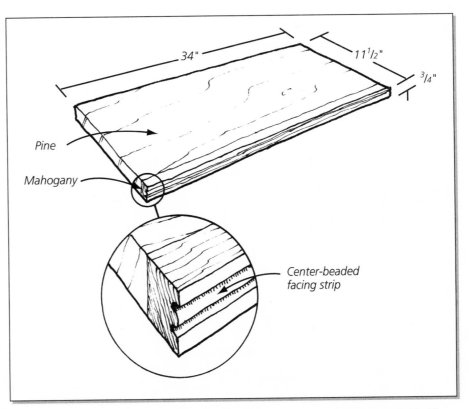

*Figure 111 Shelf details*

## CUTTING LIST

**Carcase:**

| | |
|---|---|
| 2 sides | .60½″ x 13⅜″ x ⅞″ |
| 1 top | .36¼″ x 13⅜″ x ⅞″ |

**Back:**

| | |
|---|---|
| 2 stiles | .60″ x 2½″ x ⅞″ |
| 1 top rail | .36″ x 2½″ x ⅞″ |
| 1 bottom rail | .36″ x 3″ x ⅞″ |
| 1 muntin | .36″ x 2″ x ⅞″ |
| 3 panels | .23″ x 11½″ x ½″ |
| 3 panels | .34″ x 11½″ x ½″ |
| 6 shelves (inclusive of facing strips) | .34″ x 11½″ x ¾″ |

**Doors:**

4 stiles . . . . . . . . . . . . . . . . . . . . . . . . . . . . . . . .59¾″ x 2″ x ⅞″

2 top rails . . . . . . . . . . . . . . . . . . . . . . . . . . . . . .14⅞″ x 2″ x ⅞″

2 bottom rails . . . . . . . . . . . . . . . . . . . . . . . . . . .14⅞″ x 3½″ x ⅞″

2 muntins . . . . . . . . . . . . . . . . . . . . . . . . . . . . . .14⅞″ x 1½″ x ⅞″

16 restraining strips . . . . . . . . . . . . . . . . . . . .length as needed x ¼″ x ¼″

**Stand frame:**

2 long pieces . . . . . . . . . . . . . . . . . . . . . . . . . . .40″ x 5″ x ⅞″

2 short pieces . . . . . . . . . . . . . . . . . . . . . . . . . . .20″ x 5″ x ⅞″

3 shoe pieces . . . . . . . . . . . . . . . . . . . . . . . . . . .78 inches total length x ¾″ x ¾″

4 sub-moulding pieces . . . . . . . . . . . . . . . . . . .160 inches total length
x ¾″ x ¾″

**Legs:**

4 legs . . . . . . . . . . . . . . . . . . . . . . . . . . . . . . . . .16¾″ x 4″ x 4″

8 knee blocks . . . . . . . . . . . . . . . . . . . . . . . . . .2¾″ x 2¾″ x 3″

**Top:**

1 Top moulding . . . . . . . . . . . . . . . . . . . . . . . . .80 inches total length
x 5″ x ⅞″

1 front frame piece . . . . . . . . . . . . . . . . . . . . . .36-¼″ x 4″ x ⅞″

2 side frame pieces . . . . . . . . . . . . . . . . . . . . . .20″ x 4″ x ⅞″

1 back frame piece . . . . . . . . . . . . . . . . . . . . . .35-½″ x 4″ x ⅞″

3 sub-moulding pieces . . . . . . . . . . . . . . . . . . .80 inches total length
x 1″ x ¾″

3 base-moulding pieces . . . . . . . . . . . . . . . . . .80 inches total length
x 2″ x ¼″

**Hardware:**

2 pairs of 2½-inch cabinet butts

2 2-inch barrel bolts

1 cabinet lack or latch

½ gross #8 x 1¼-inch-flat-head woodscrews

1 box restraining strip brads

24 shelf supports

# Gothic armchair

*Exploring different mind-sets*

High-style antique furniture has always fascinated me as much for its excellence as for the way in which it was made. To admire a Louis XV bombé desk, resplendent in all its exotically veneered curvaceousness, encrusted with gilt-bronze mounts, and topped with exquisitely veined rose marble, always begs the question of how such fine work was done in shops and with tools that today strike us as so primitive.

Nowadays, when every weekend woodworker has a shop equipped with tablesaws, routers, and plate-joiners, competent woodworking seems to require an ever greater attention to precision: setting up jointer knives, finely tuning tablesaw fences, and calibrating runout with micrometers. Even the simplest joinery is approached with an astonishing array of high-tech jigs. To consider the construction of even the simplest piece made in previous centuries without all this power and technology is almost inconceivable. But attempting to replicate something radically different from the kind of thing you are most familiar with can be an extremely useful exercise. It can enrich your design vocabulary with previously unthought-of forms and techniques.

The Gothic armchair is a copy of a chair made, so far as anyone knows, sometime in the fifteenth century. The records are scant. The accession slip in the Metropolitan Museum of Art where the chair now stands in the dimly lit hall of medieval furniture notes only that it was given to the museum by J. Pierpont Morgan in 1916, and came from the Hoentschel collection in Paris. It is described as French, but may very well have been made in Flanders, where similar work was produced.

At first I was impressed only by the chair's dark and massive presence. But every time I passed by, on my way to the better lit area where the eighteenth-century American masterpieces are kept, I found myself looking closer and closer. The chair was so old and alien in form, so different from anything having to do with contemporary woodworking, that I couldn't help thinking about the wood-worker who had made it and how it had been done.

The back, made high to impress, keep out the draft, and protect against attacks from the rear, was rough hewn, showing the ax or hatchet marks plainly, but the front of the paneling was carved in elegant linenfold, and there was a pierced tracery panel at the top of the back flanked by crockets, a frequent medieval carved motif representing curled leaves and buds. At the time it was made chairs were rare and reserved for the richest and most powerful. This had been a very important item, possibly belonging to a bishop or feudal lord; a veritable throne. Despite the fact that the gloomy ambience lent an undeniable feeling of extreme age and made it easy to imagine its original setting in some dark northern European castle, the fact is that these pieces were most usually originally brightly painted and often covered with rich fabric for comfort and color. Over the centuries the paint has worn off and the wood become smoke blackened, and we now equate Gothic furniture with somber oak pieces, almost ebony in appearance.

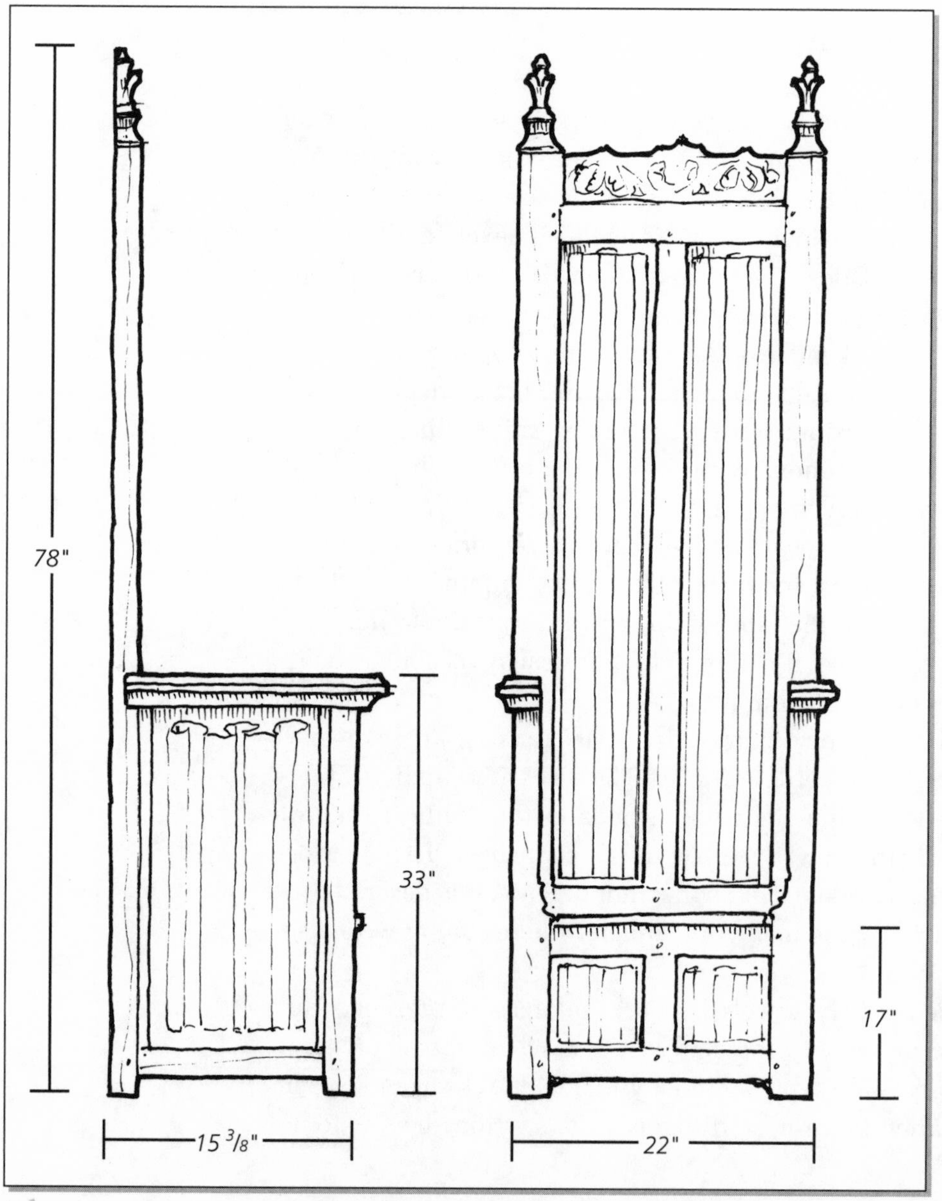

I looked closer each time, and eventually I made a number of sketches, noting as many details as possible. It became apparent that this was no rude construction; there were aspects of considerable subtlety, and despite a somewhat presbyopic and cavalier attention to the sort of detail that concerns us so greatly today—the perfect fit of every joint and the immaculate finish of every surface—the chair radiated an authority and splendor that could have been produced only by someone very sensitive and sure of his craft. And all this was done with no tablesaw, no router, no tenoning jig, no electricity. . . .

I at last decided to make my own chair, and embarked on a voyage of rediscovery that at times made me feel very close to that anonymous fifteenth-century woodworker as I tried to solve the same problems and think the

*Figure 112 Overall dimensions*

same way as he must have done, working as close to the vernacular of the time as possible. My dimensions (*Figure 112*) do not duplicate those of the original exactly; I was not able to get close enough to take precise measurements, and in any case I am sure the original units were not in feet and inches. Although I tried to preserve the relative proportions of the parts, I allowed my material to dictate the exact size of the various members, as I am sure did the original maker.

The following directions will bring you very close to duplicating the manufacture of a major piece of furniture of the fifteenth century, and at the same time may surprise you with both their sophistication and the realization of how much contemporary woodworking owes to these ancient woodworkers. Styles may change but the material remains the same, as do many of the ways of working it.

**Materials**—Oak and walnut were commonly used in this period, but because both species change color considerably with age—not to mention the fact that much medieval furniture was either painted or covered with painted canvas—there seems little reason not to use any medium-density hardwood that may be carved fairly crisply.

**Construction**—The entire chair, except for the hinged seat, is made using frame-and-panel construction, and virtually all the joinery is mortise-and-tenon. The job may be broken into three parts: making the framed sections; carving the panels, including the pierced section at the top of the back; and assembly, including fitting the seat and making the floor of the box under the seat.

**The framing**—The framework for the back is similar to that of a paneled door and consists of two vertical stiles, three rails (bottom, seat, and top), and two muntins. The front is similarly constructed with two stiles forming the front legs and arm supports, connected by two rails that, together with a short vertical muntin, enclose the front panels. The front is joined to the back by the arms, the seat rails, which do not interrupt the side panels but run along their inside surface, and the bottom rails (*Figure 113*).

Figure 113 Framing dimensions

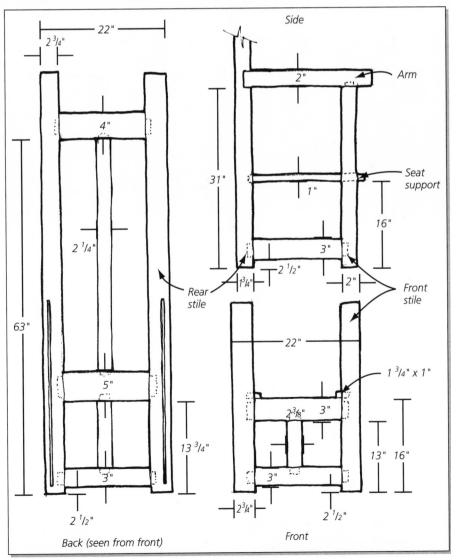

It seems a little perverse to reduce lumber that is already more prepared than was readily available in the fifteenth century to a more primitive state by duplicating the rough-hewn surfaces of the original's back and nether surfaces. Instead, begin by preparing all the above-mentioned parts, to the given dimensions, to be as straight and as square as possible.

Note that several members need to be initially prepared larger than the finished dimensions to accommodate subsequent shaping. These are: the tops of the rear stiles, which will be carved into crocketed finials; the arms, which will be coved top and bottom on their outside and front surfaces; and the front stiles, which will be reduced above the seat level after a carved transition. Be sure also to leave extra length for the various tenons needed on the muntins, rails, arms, upper ends of the front stiles, and both ends of the seat support.

A special word about the arms: the outsides do not run all the way to a point flush with the back of the rear stiles. This is because their tenons must stop short of the groove formed in the inside of the stiles in order to allow the back panels to seat properly, and it is easier to cut the end of the tenon and the end of the outside portion of the arm to the same length. It is, however, important to make this tenon quite as long as possible in order to provide ample area for the pin that will secure the tenon.

Cut the mortises necessary to receive these tenons after forming the grooves needed to receive the various panels. This will ensure that the mortises and grooves line up as is normal and most convenient in frame-and-panel work. Note, however, that the grooves in the front stiles which will receive the front panels stop at the height of the front top rail. Be sure to lay out the stopped grooves in the front of the rear stiles, which will receive the side panels, to align properly with the grooves in the side bottom rails. Laying out the arms requires careful attention because at the start none of their prepared faces will be flush with any other face of either the front or the rear stile. For similar reasons it is best to lay out the mortises for the seat supports after the rest of the framing has been temporarily dry-assembled.

Finally, remember to form a rabbet along the inside top edge of the seat supports to receive the matching rabbeted edge of the seat (*Figure 114*), as well as along the bottom corner of the bottom rails to receive the floor of the seat box. The photograph shows the assembled framing knocked together dry and unpinned, grooved to receive the paneling, but as yet unformed or carved.

**Shaping and moulding the framing**—All front inside edges of framing members enclosing panels are chamfered. The chamfers meet in mason's miters, which are square-cornered at the bottom and curved at

*Figure 114 Front stile reduction and seat support joint*

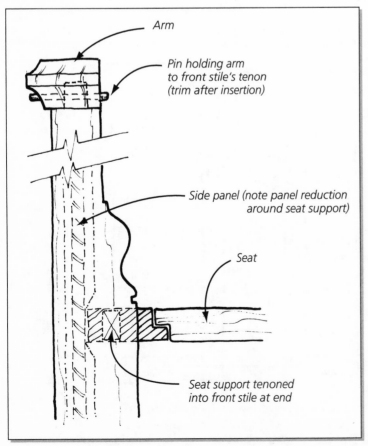

Arm

Pin holding arm to front stile's tenon (trim after insertion)

Side panel (note panel reduction around seat support)

Seat

Seat support tenoned into front stile at end

the top, except at the top of the side panels, where the overhanging arm precludes the forming of a chamfer, and where the chamfers on the uprights run up to the underneath of the arm at the front, and are stopped a little below it at the back (*Figure 115*). When making the mason's miters, note that the horizontal chamfers on the rails can be run to the end of the member, but the chamfers on the vertical members should be stopped at the level of the abutting rail and the corner then finished after the frame is assembled to ensure a smooth transition.

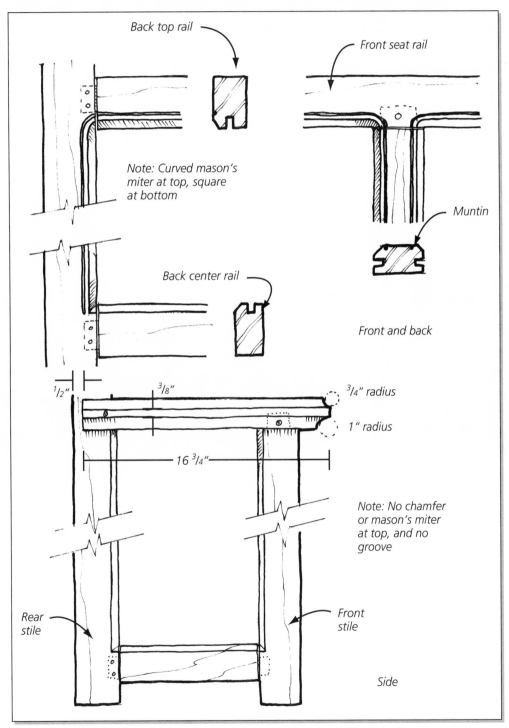

Figure 115
Chamfering details

Similarly, the narrow groove that outlines the chamfer at the sides and top must also be formed after the framing is assembled to ensure a smooth continuity. You may be tempted to form these chamfers, miters, and grooves mechanically, but it is readily apparent from their irregularity that the originals were cut freehand. It is not the perfection of the details but the overall robustness of an integrated design that gives the chair its power and presence.

When chamfering the rear stiles, be aware of two important details: the upper end of the chamfer is stopped square at the top, and a drop is formed in the corner.

Next, reduce the thickness of the upper part of the front stiles so that their inside surfaces are flush with the inside faces of the arms. The variously curved transition section just above the seat may be cut with a bandsaw or, as was probably done on the original, by making several deep cuts with a backsaw and chiseling out the waste, fairing the profile with rasps and files.

The upper and lower coves formed on the outside and front edges of the arms are not equal! They may be started as bevels and then hollowed with gouges or, more easily, by using a round plane. Whatever method you employ, form the coves on the front, across the grain, first. Any chipping or splitting that might occur at the sides will then be removed as the side coves are formed.

*Figure 116 Finial
details*

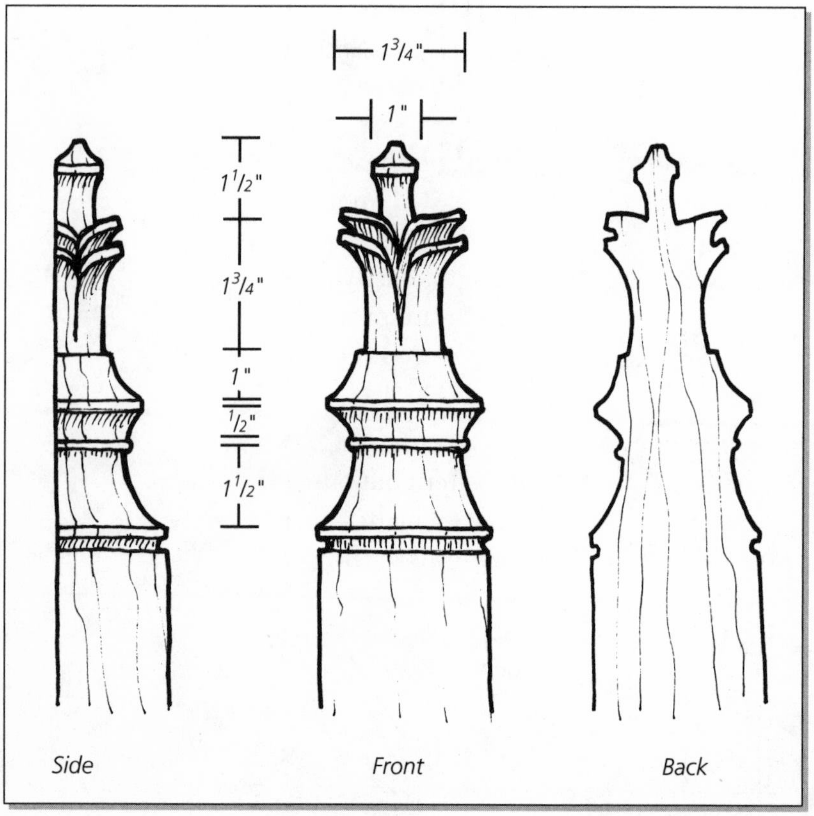

Side

Front

Back

Last, carve the crocketed finials (*Figure 116*). Be bold, do not worry about perfection. Saw close to the profile with a narrow-bladed saw and remove the waste with carving tools. Cut the defining lines between the leaves last. Be sure only to keep the heights of the various leaves and the tops of the finials and the lower protrusions equal on both stiles.

**The panels**—Nine panels are needed: the wide, pierced carved panel at the top of the chair; two side panels; two front panels; and four back panels, of which only the two longer upper ones are carved, the lower pair being simply fielded on both sides. The original panels were all single pieces, and I was fortunate to have lumber wide enough to duplicate this, but there is no reason why you may not make up individual panels from several narrower widths.

Start by cutting the panels to size so that they will fit in their grooves with enough room for any possible expansion. This is more important across the width than in the length; ideally the grooves should be deep enough that if the panels shrink they will still be wide enough for their edges to remain hidden in the grooves.

Now feather the backs gently to define a rectangular field. This was done very coarsely on the original; the concern seems to have been only for fit, not for appearance. Note that the backs of the side panels form the inside of the seat area

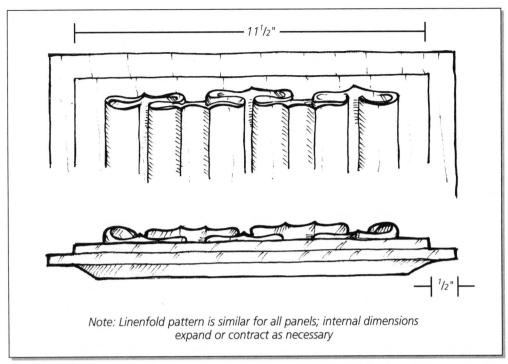

Note: Linenfold pattern is similar for all panels; internal dimensions expand or contract as necessary

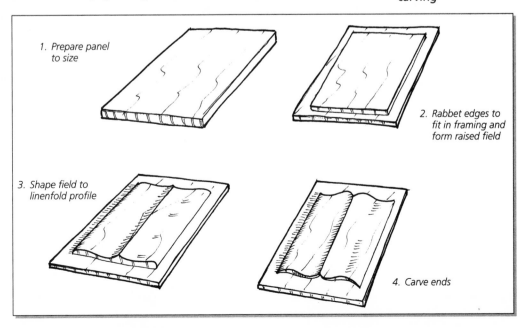

*Figure 117 Linenfold pattern*

and must be formed with an additional depression across their width at the point where the seat supports will butt up against them.

Lay out the areas to be carved into linenfold and cut rabbets on these surfaces extending to the edges of the linenfold area and to a depth that will produce an edge thin enough to fit in the grooves in the framing.

The linenfold pattern is the same for all panels (*Figure 117*). It is easily produced using traditional ploughs and grooving planes to form the hollows and then rounding the curves with hollows and rounds, or by using various router bits, carving the ends with appropriate gouges.

**Preparing the linenfold paneling**—There are innumerable variations of linenfold paneling; those used in the Gothic chair duplicate the original pattern but other, simpler patterns can be used. The process is essentially the same no matter how many "folds" are involved in any given panel, so it is easiest to describe the

*Figure 118 Linenfold carving*

process using the basic single fold. Once you have formed such a panel, designing more complicated examples is simply a matter of repeating the steps outlined below. The process, as shown in *Figure 118*, consists of four steps:

1. Prepare panel to size

2. Rabbet edges to fit in framing and form raised field

3. Shape field to linenfold profile

4. Carve ends

1. Prepare a panel to the right overall size to fit in the grooved framework that will receive the completed linenfold panel.

2. Rabbet the edges so that the reduced thickness of the panel's edge will fit in the framework's grooves, leaving the center of the panel thereby raised.

3. Shape this raised center portion of the panel so as to form the undulating folds.

4. Carve the top and bottom ends of the now shaped panel to represent the way the "linen" folds over on itself.

**Shaping the folds**—Steps 1 and 2 should present no problems provided you remember to size the panel to allow for the usual expansion and contraction of panels within grooves, and provided you make the width of the rabbet sufficient to place the raised portion of the panel at least ½ inch or more in from the inside edges of the framing. If the panel needs to be made up of several boards in order to achieve the needed width, make sure to align the constituent boards so that the grain is running in the same direction. This will make planing the folds easier.

The usual instructions given are first to plow grooves the length of the panel corresponding to the future hollows. This is hard to do with handtools such as plough planes since the hollows are often too far from the edge of the panel to allow the tool's fence to be used. A tablesaw is not much help either, since the groove made with a regular blade is too narrow and the groove made by a dado headset is too wide. Using a router can be similarly impracticable given the amount of setup needed. Much easier than any of these methods is to pencil in a few rough guidelines and begin with any round plane less than ¾ inch wide at the deepest points of the future hollows, where grooves might be recommended.

Once the round plane has formed these small grooves, the procedure is to widen the grooves until their inside edges meet in a sharp arris at the center of the panel. Use a round plane between ¾ inch and 1¼ inches wide in such a way that the groove is widened but not deepened. This is achieved by tilting the plane sideways; the groove will be widened on that side opposite to the plane's tilt (*Figure 119*). Using only your fingers as a fence to guide the round plane—or even moving the plane completely freehand—you will be surprised how nicely you will be able to work gradually closer to the center line and eventually produce a remarkably straight arris. Remember, this is carving, not precision joinery.

*Figure 119 Forming concave sections of profile*

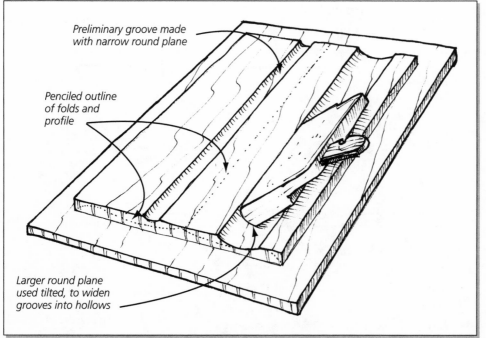

Preliminary groove made with narrow round plane

Penciled outline of folds and profile

Larger round plane used tilted, to widen grooves into hollows

To shape the edges of the depressions where they rise to the surface and turn into the convex portion of the fold, a block plane will suffice. Where the rounded-over portion of the profile doubles back on itself, a certain amount of undercutting is necessary. This can be greatly emphasized if you possess specialist planes such as side rabbets or snipesbills, but an ordinary hollow plane about ¾ inch wide will produce enough of a curve for a satisfactory profile (*Figure 120*). Note only that you cannot form a rounded-over profile with a hollow plane narrower than the desired profile or the edges of its cutting iron will cut into the curve.

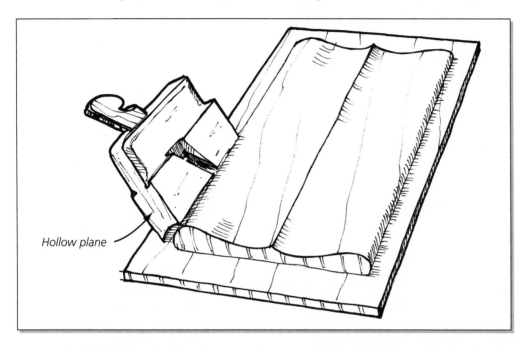

*Figure 120 Forming convex sections of linenfold*

Once the basic profile has been formed, a little ingenuity with side rabbet planes, including the common metal versions made by Stanley, or a gentle gouge will produce sufficient undercutting at the edges of the folded-over portions of the profile.

**Carving the ends**—One or two simple carving gouges are all that is needed here. The secret for success is first to pencil the required finished outline on both the top *and* the end of the panel.

Two patterns are illustrated. The first, for a simple single-fold panel, requires only vertical cuts, which may be made using appropriately shaped gouges (*Figure 121*). Most linenfold panels have a fairly shallow profile, so the vertical cuts required even at the highest points of the fold will not be very deep. The usual technique used by carvers to form outlines, using a V-shaped parting tool to describe the outline, and then deepening the cut with a gouge, can make life a little easier.

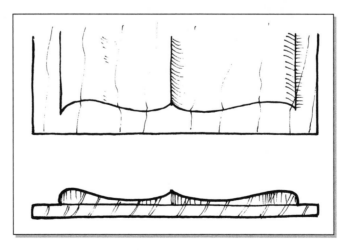

*Figure 121 End profile of single fold*

The second pattern is very similar to that used on the Gothic chair (*Figure 122*). When starting work on the still-square ends, confusion can be avoided if you work first from the top of the panel, cutting in the required outline, but keeping an eye on the end so that none of the downward cuts goes deeper than the level of the various folds. In fact, if you first reduce the height of the wood to these various levels, the subsequent shaping of their outlines as seen from the top of the panel will be easily understood.

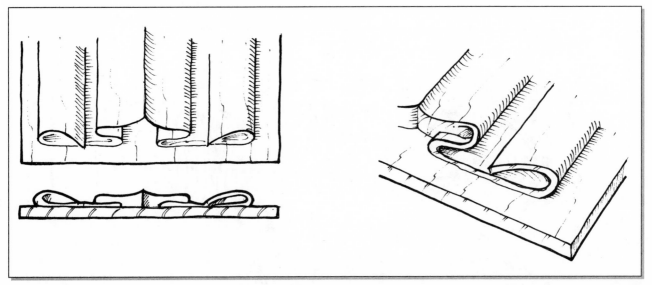

*Figure 122 Gothic armchair linenfold*

To enhance the effect once the basic outline has been formed, a little judicious undercutting at those points where the "linen" folds over itself is effective; just pay attention not to remove any material that should form part of any inferior folds.

**Additional patterns**—Linenfold paneling is by no means unknown in many older buildings and churches in larger American cities, and many museums have examples of furniture of the oak period, such as the Gothic chair itself in the New York Metropolitan Museum of Art. It is quite common in older buildings in Europe, and there are many good books illustrating different examples. The varieties are endless; there is a room in Hampton Court Palace in England completely paneled with linenfold, no two panels of which are alike!

**Preparing the pierced panel**—Carving the pierced panel is not difficult if the pattern (*Figure 123*) is first carefully drawn on the panel. Because the panel needs to be thick enough to accommodate the beveling and lower-level cusping described below, it will be necessary to form a rabbet on the back edge of the sides in order to allow it to fit in the grooves in the inside of the stiles. The bottom of the panel sits on the top edge of the top rail with no groove or corresponding tongue.

Bore holes large enough to receive the blade of a coping saw, a fretsaw, or even a narrow keyhole saw in the corners of the pierced parts and saw these sections out, cleaning up the corners and fairing the insides with chisels. The front edges are all beveled, leaving an even band at the front, from which the triangular cusps that protrude into the pierced areas, sometimes meeting each other, emerge at a somewhat lower level. A small recessed triangle is cut in the interior of all the cusps, and the two unpierced triangles at the top are decorated with low-relief oak leaves, the background to which is stippled with punch marks made with the point of a fairly large nail or a metal nail set. All openings at the back of the panel are lightly chamfered.

**Assembly**—Assemble the various panels without glue into their respective framing, gluing and pinning the tenons as follows: First glue and assemble the back, and then glue and assemble the two sides, sliding the side panels into the incom-

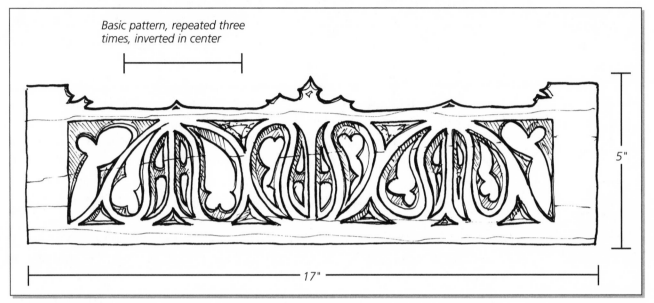

Figure 123 Pierced panel

plete, three-part frames formed by the front leg, bottom side rail, and arm. Now assemble the two front panels into the framing formed by the seat and bottom rails and their connecting central muntin. When this part is assembled, fix the brackets shown at *Figure 124* and join the completed front to the two previously assembled sides.

Before assembling the now complete front-and-side unit to the back, insert the front ends of the seat supports into their mortises in the back of the front legs. The horizontal depression formed across the center of each side panel will help to keep the seat supports somewhat level, but an extra pair of hands to help guide their back ends into the back legs, as well as seat the back edge of the side panels in their respective grooves, will make this part of the assembly a lot easier.

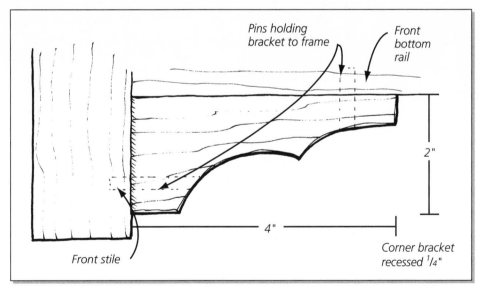

Figure 124 Bottom bracket

Draw all tenons close with clamps if necessary, and bore for the pins. If clamping and boring are too unwieldy, you may prefer to draw-bore the mortise-and-tenon joinery by boring for the pins only through the mortises; inserting the tenons and marking them with an awl inserted through the holes bored in the mortises; and then boring the tenons slightly off center, towards the shoulders. This will cause the pins when inserted to draw the joints tight.

The pins should be made from square stock whose four corners are chamfered to create an octagonal pin. Make one end slightly smaller so that each pin can be started in its hole, and then drive them home with a mallet. Any protruding ends should be planed flush. No glue is necessary. Indeed, any glue used on the mortise-and-tenon joinery in the original may well have long since failed with little effect on the chair's integrity since the pinning, in combination with the shouldered tenons, is more than sufficient to hold the framing firmly together. The panels and the seat-box floor will in turn maintain squareness.

**The seat**—The original seat consists of a single board, rabbeted underneath at the sides only, to fit into the rabbeted seat support, and attached to the seat rail in the back by two large pairs of iron staples. The crudeness of this hardware has been tempered by the patina of centuries and is probably best replaced by a pair of unobtrusive butt hinges mortised into the back edge of the seat and then attached to the seat rail. By leaving the flooring of the box—which consists simply of rough boards nailed into the rabbets formed in the bottom edges of the framing under the chair—to the last step, attaching the seat is made a little easier.

The original chair's seat is secured by a large lock mortised into the front's top rail, but this appears to have been a later addition and may be included or omitted as you desire.

**Finishing**—There are traces of color in the crevices of the original indicating a polychromatic finish typical of much medieval furniture, as well as series of nail holes around the arms indicating the use of attached fabric for color or cushioning. But a simple oil finish, or even a coat of wax, is all that is needed to afford minimum protection to the chair. A few centuries of being dragged from smoky castle to smoky castle will effect its own patina. The original bears a multitude of scars and dents suggesting a rich history, but neither these nor the rough simplicity of the overall construction detracts one bit from a magnificent presence.

## CUTTING LIST

**Back frame:**

| | |
|---|---|
| 2 stiles | 78″ x 2¾″ x 1¾″ |
| 1 top rail | 19½″ x 4″ x 1¾″ |
| 1 seat rail | 19½″ x 5″ x 1¾″ |
| 1 top muntin | 45½″ x 2¼″ x 1¾″ |
| 1 bottom muntin | 11¾″ x 2¼″ x 1¾″ |
| 2 top panels | 45¼″ x 7½″ x ¾″ |
| 2 bottom panels | 9½″ x 7½″ x ¾″ |
| 1 pierced panel | 17″ x 5″ |

**Front frame:**

| | |
|---|---|
| 2 stiles | 32½″ x 2¾″ x 2″ |
| 2 rails | 19½″ x 3″ x 1¾″ |
| 1 muntin | 11″ x 2⅜″ x 1¾″ |
| 2 panels | 11½″ x 7½″ x ¾″ |
| 2 bottom brackets | 4″ x 2″ x 2″ |

**Sides:**

2 arms  . . . . . . . . . . . . . . . . . . . . . . . . . . . . .16¾″ x 2″ x 2″
2 panels  . . . . . . . . . . . . . . . . . . . . . . . . . . . .26″ x 12″
2 seat supports  . . . . . . . . . . . . . . . . . . . . . .15½″ x 1″ x 2-½″
1 seat  . . . . . . . . . . . . . . . . . . . . . . . . . . . . . .16″ x 14″ x ¾″
40 pins  . . . . . . . . . . . . . . . . . . . . . . . . . . . . . .2″ x ½-inch diameter

**Hardware:**

2 2-inch butt hinges

# Index